I0463247

Wedding Photographer

"Photograph Weddings Like The Pros"

Learn digital wedding photography.

Wedding Photography tips, ideas, and poses.

Photographing your first wedding.

Create an affordable wedding photography business.

By David M Graubard

www.WeddingPhotographerBook.com

Wedding Photographer

"Photograph Weddings Like The Pros"

Learn digital wedding photography.

Wedding Photography tips, ideas, and poses.

Photographing your first wedding.

Create an affordable wedding photography business.

By David M Graubard

Graubard, David M.
Wedding Photographer Book
"Photograph A Wedding Like The Pros"
1.Wedding Photography 2.Photography I. Title
II. Title Wedding Photographer Book
778.993

Contact info go to;
www.WeddingPhotographerBook.com

You miss 100% of the shots you don't take.
-Wayne Gretzky
Professional Hockey Player

Dedication;
I dedicated this book to my wife Tara, and the boys,
Joshua and Jonah, Say cheese…………

Thank you,
To all of my clients that have made my business
a great success

TABLE OF CONTENTS

INTRODUCTION

You can do it! You can take beautiful images and have fun doing it! I have seen more and more financially responsible couples using alternative methods of having their wedding photos taken.   Technology today has allowed many amateurs and hobbyists photographers to jump into wedding photography.   Many of the basic Camera's on today's market are capable of taking professional images. Most likely you already have the equipment necessary but just needs some basic guidance from a wedding photographer professional.

I hope that you will have as much joy as I have had in photographing weddings. Photographing a friend's wedding was one of the best gifts I have ever given. Wedding photography can be simple as long as the basics are known. My goal is not to only get the photographer through the wedding but to blow away the other photographers in the room. The photographer that reads this book will have the "wow" power, so that people that view these images will keep asking who took them.

Wedding Photography

When I jumped into professional Photography I was frustrated by the lack of available books discussing the very basics of wedding photography. Most of the wedding photography books on the market are about operating a well established large studio photo business. I wrote this book to fill the need for basic wedding photography . I felt that the "pros" were out of touch. The "pros" were giving an exclusive appearance. Ironically, most of the wedding photographers do not own studio's they operate "on location". In addition the pro's denial of turning over the wedding photos in digital format to the bride and holding exclusive copyrights is supporting my claim that the "pros" lack vision. The married couple needs to have their images back to do what they want with them. Enlargements, duplications, uploads to social networks, and more. The old days of expensive darkrooms and high cost processing are over. The regular person now has the same access as the professional in completing the final product without the large markup. I will discuss in detail the equipment recommended, the order of the wedding day, poses, creative wedding photography, and tips. This book gives the photographer the tools they need to succeed in wedding photography.

Equipment

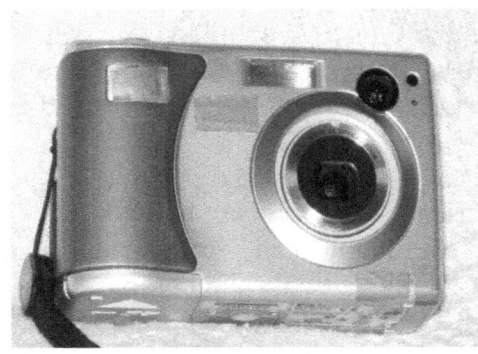

There are three popular types of camera bodies. Point and shoot, SLR "Style", and Single lens reflex (SLR). The point and shoot camera is usually not used as a primary wedding photographer. Point and shoot camera's may have a high mega pixel number but lack a large enough internal senor to absorbed enough light for better clarity. Hopefully one of the next kind of cameras are available for the wedding. This will improve the image quality.

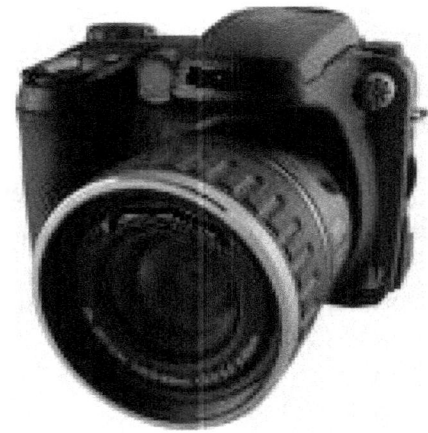

Some weddings are photographed by the SLR "style". The SLR "style" camera has a larger body than the point and shoot with a bigger lens but again sometimes lack a large enough sensor. There are some SLR "style" camera's with larger sensors and are competitive to the next class of cameras.

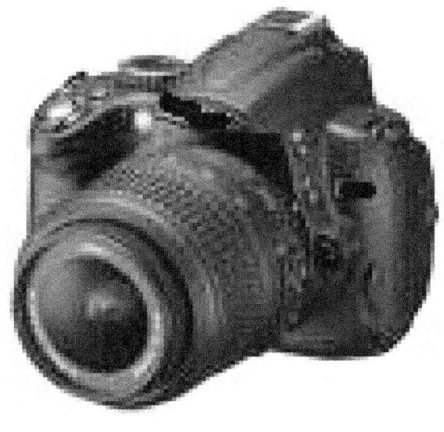

Most weddings are photographed with a SLR. The SLR has a large sensor to work well in a low light condition. The primary reason for the SLR is the access to multiple lens and an external flash capability.

The camera industry has made it easy by selling a SLR kit with a "walk around" lens. Fortunately the "walk around" lens is perfect for weddings. This lens has the ability to zoom in for close up and go wide for a group photo. The SLR "style" camera has been becoming popular since they come with the "walk around" lens permanently attached.

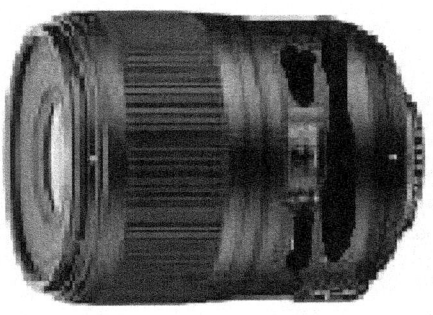

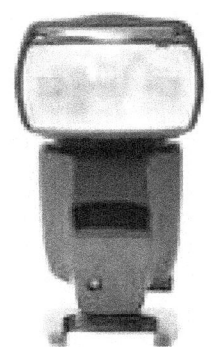

The external flash is one of the most important parts of the professional photographer's arsenal. This is why the point and shoot camera may be lacking. The small flash on a point and shoot camera may be insufficient in lighting up the scene. There are plenty of inexpensive external flash options that will help brighten up a dimly light banquet hall. Every SLR has a top mounted port for an external flash. Unfortunately the flash is what causes the "red eye" photos. The " red eye" is caused by a direct bounce of the flash against the eye of the photographed person back to the camera's lens. To minimize this "red eye" the external flash needs to be moved father way from the lens (the bounced flash will not come directly back to the lens.) This is done by attaching a Flash sync cord. As long as the flask is at least 7" from the lens, the chance of "red eye" is greatly diminished. Some photographer's hand hold the flash in one hand and the and the camera in the other hand. This can be tricky so the best method is to mount the flash on a Flash Bracket that is attached to the base of the cameras.

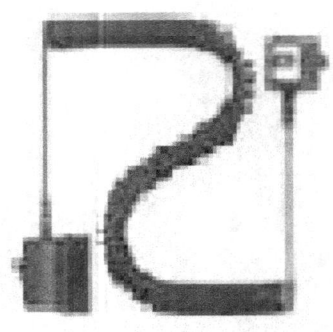

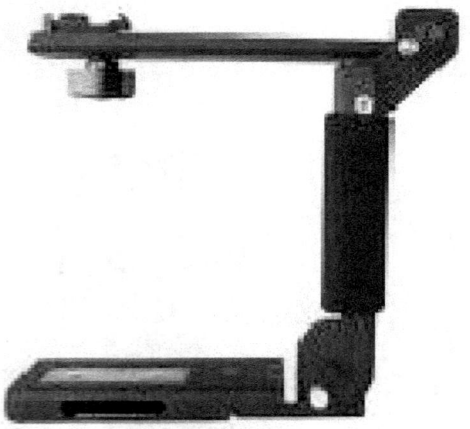

There are many bracket styles available but I like the lightest one I can find and this is usually the least costly. The flash should also be used outdoors to keep away shadows from covering the subject's face. Flash technology is very simple. The camera has a Through the Lens(TTL) sensor. That has a cover called the shutter. When the correct amount of light goes through the lens, the shutter closes. The more light that you have the quicker the shutter closes. If you have less light the shutter stays open longer until the correct amount of light is achieved at the sensor.

Accessories-batteries, filters, sd cards, lens cleaner

Each camera will need to have fully charged batteries and fully charged backups. The average wedding could have over 300 photos. With the power of the flash and all day shooting the batteries may become depleted. Extra memory cards are a must. Make sure to format the memory cards before the wedding because it is never a good idea to start erasing memory cards during a wedding, especially if the wrong memory card gets erased. The camera lens must be kept clean at all times. It is easier to clean a lens that has a clear filter attached. If the filter cannot be cleaned then change or remove the filter. Always keep lens/filter cleaning equipment nearby.

Back up gear

A professional photographer is a person that earns a living by taking photos. MY definition of a professional photographer is a person that takes photos and has back up gear. For a photographer starting out this may be the biggest financial hurdle. Have some kind of back up gear, even having to borrow a point and shoot camera for the day just in case. It seems to me that if you have back up gear everything runs smoothly, no back up gear and anything can go wrong. In my professional wedding career, up to this point I rarely have had any equipment problems. The only problem I had was accidentally using an old battery. The backup gear allowed me to get to a part of the wedding were I had time to figure out what the problem was. In addition backup gear has always given me mental relief that if my equipment was damaged during the wedding I could still carry on.

Camera Technical operation

I recommend running the camera on full auto. Photographers can waste valuable time and opportunities trying to play with the settings. Early in my career I read an article by a high end wedding photographer stating that he was photographing in full auto and concentrating on composition. I agree, this frees up time on taking the best images and then if needed tweak the photos in a photo imaging software. Some of the best photos in news media were not the best of quality but the timing was perfect, possibly once in a lifetime. Especially with basic photo editing software these images can be improved. To better understand full auto is to think about the millions of dollars the camera's manufactures have put in to technology and hiring the best engineers to get your camera to take the best images. Leave the camera on auto and relax.

Shot Sheet

Before every wedding I prepare a shot sheet. A shot sheet is one piece of paper that lists photos that I have to create in addition to the regular order of the wedding. Remember most of the wedding is photography in journalistic style with very little input from the photographer.

Try to avoid the Martha Stewart's list of formal images, this is a large list of every person in the wedding in multiple combinations . The list is daunting and can become overwhelming not only for the photographer but the bride and groom. Instead make a short list of poses. In addition to the list of poses, I have some small images of poses that I like. The poses lists and images give me plenty of ideas through out the wedding on taking exciting images. When I started out these images were of poses that I saw on the internet. I simply copied and pasted them on my shot sheet for a quick and easy reference. I keep this shot sheet on me the entire day so it allows me to free up my mind. I can concentrate on taking photos and not trying to remember what's next.

Example of Shot Sheet;

Shot Sheet
Photo of b-man w/rings

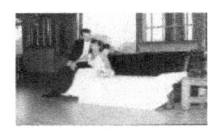
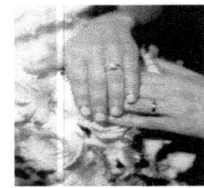

Formals
Bride and Groom
B and G w/ Both sets of Parents /Grand Parents
Grooms Men plus best man alone (wide)
Bride's maids plus maid of honor alone (low angle)
FULL WEDDING PARTY

Informal
RING SHOT !!!
FULL body Thank-you

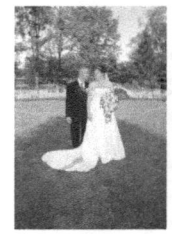

Looking at camera looking and each other
Close-up hugging w/blurred filter
Seated- g on armrest full and close

Bride hugging from behind g-seated
SILOHOUTTE OPERTUNITIES
Close-up brides flowers covering
Dance pose, left hand on his chest looking back
Groom behind looking at each other

Brides request_____
_____

Grooms request_____
_____

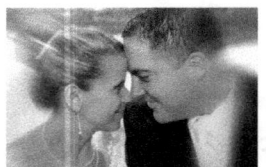

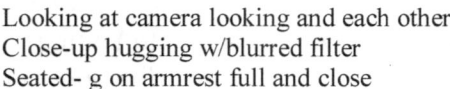
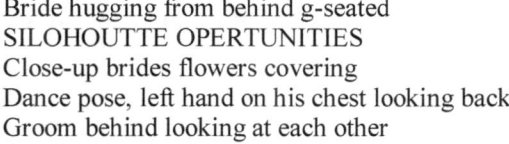

Notice that the Shot Sheet is just bullet abbreviations to help remind the photographer on poses that could be set up. I usually just fold it and keep it in my back pocket. I refer to it through out the wedding to keep me on point.

Preparation

A couple of days prior to the wedding I do a thorough equipment check and charging of the batteries. All gear is inspected and the lenses are cleaned. I also format the memory cards and make sure that the camera is set to all of the correct settings. I take care of anything that I can do this day instead of the wedding day and prepare a wedding day equipment check list.

Example of an Equipment Check list

Check List

Documentation
> Shot Sheet, Invitation, contract

Camera
> Nikon D60 w/ battery, D70s w/Battery

Lens
> 16-85mm, 17-70mm

Flash
> Nikon SB-800, sb600,

Tripod
Lens cleaning kit
Batteries
> Multiple AA's

Digital card
> (2) SD 4gb cards for d60
> (3) Compact Flash Formatted (pressing Format twice)

Camera Bags (2)
Flash Bracket with Flash Cord
Fanny Pack
Filters
> Soft 67mm

Set Up D60
> 1. All camera manuals
> 2. Focus spot
> 3. RAW

THE WEDDING DAY

On the morning of the wedding I go over the equipment check list. I turn on the camera with the flash and take my first picture which is of the wedding contract, business card or anything written down that could trace the images back to you. This is an old film trick, when the photo labs would produce hundreds of photos and if there was film missing they could find yours. Even with these removable memory cards a person who finds it could return it to you.
I gather all necessary documents, contact information, directions and equipment and keep them in a secure place.

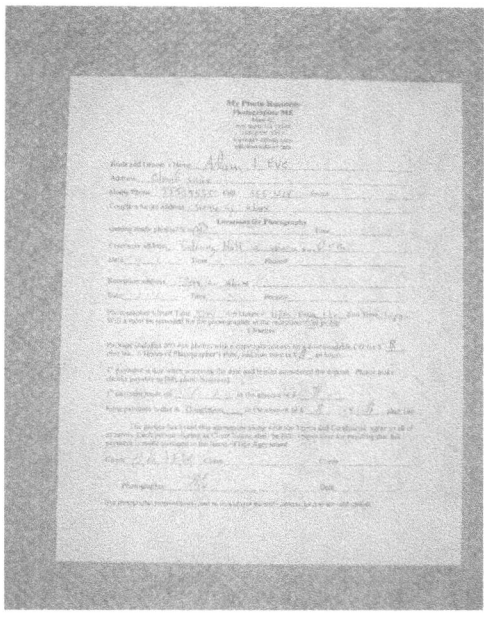

Getting Ready Photos

When the bride gets ready at the same place were the ceremony is held this is an optimal situation. Brides that are getting ready one place and driving to the ceremony at another place can be difficult for the photographer since we like to be early to all events. Many times the bride opt out of getting ready photos since many photographer are paid by time. It may seem impractical to start the photographer at the getting ready time and basically paying for the photographer's time to drive to the ceremony. The photos at this point should be primarily photojournalistic. Photos of the dress and shoes alone are classics. In addition it is important to get the mother and the bride in an image. Pros usually find an available mirror and have the bride look back at the photographer thru the mirror image. Another image is the mother setting the vial or hair piece. A group shot of the bridesmaids cam save time latter.

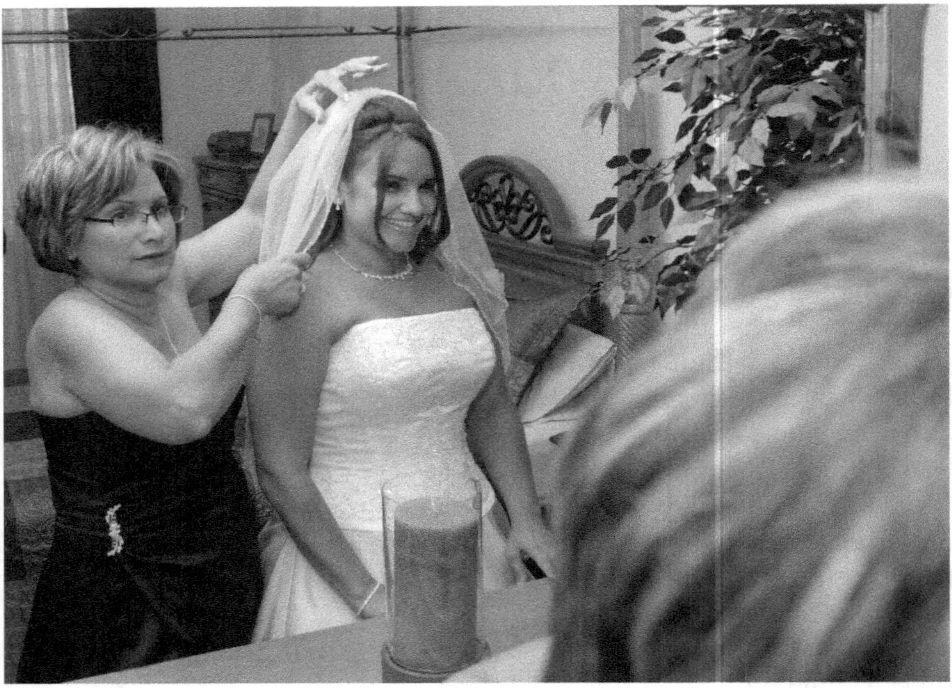

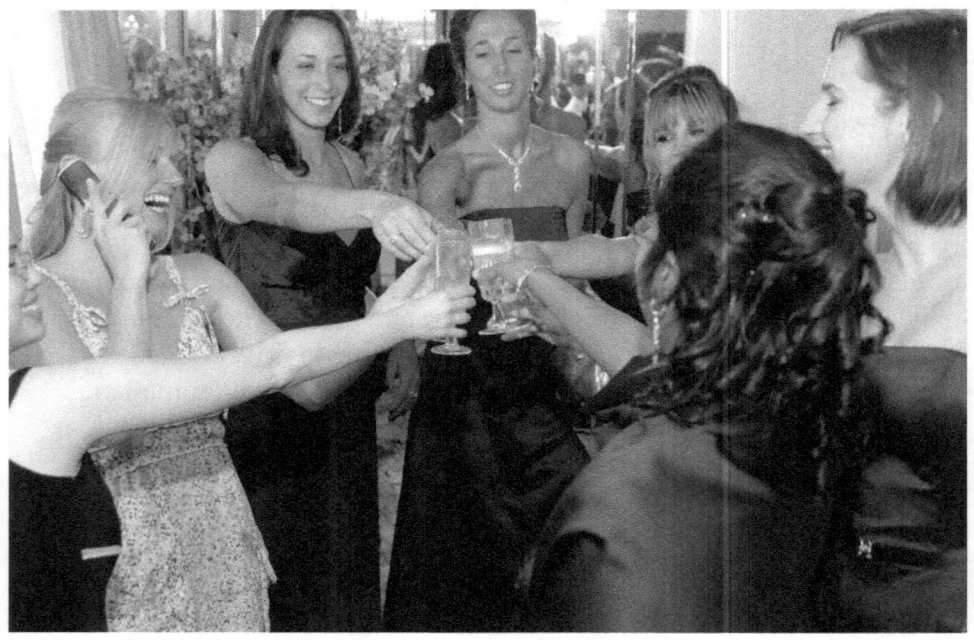

Upper Photo is a reflection image

Bride getting ready.

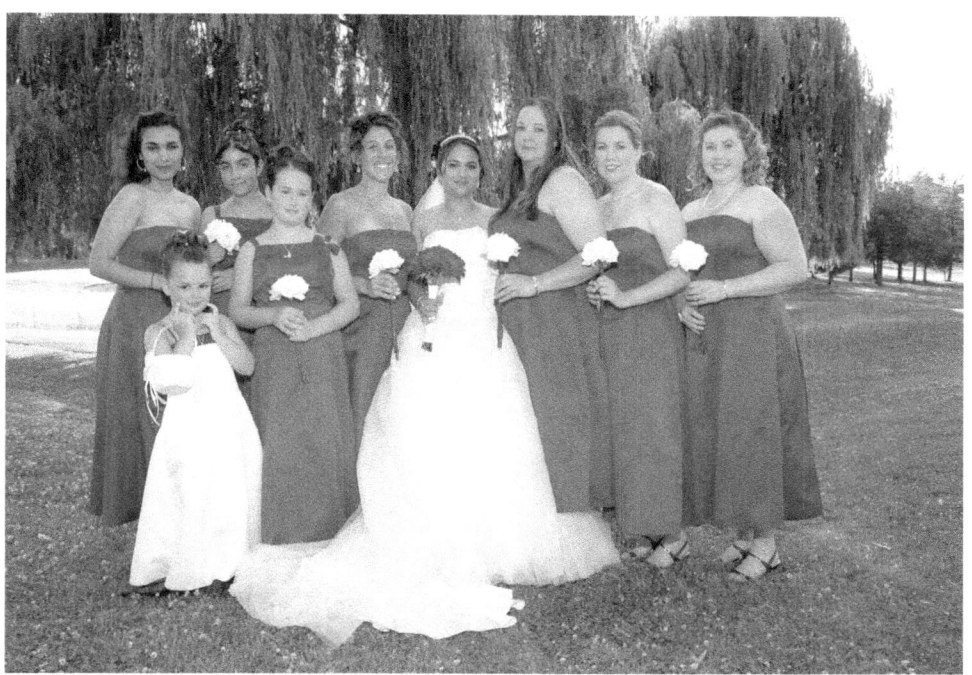

Pre-Ceremony

You will want to show up at the ceremony area early and walk around. Look for good background photo opportunities and a safe place to keep your equipment . If photographing in a church bring bottled water. There is usually no air conditioning. If it is raining, the ceremony area may be the best place for formals. The next set of photos are usually of the groomsmen, introduce yourself to the groom. Ask him about the boutonnieres and have someone put them on while you are taking their photos. These are the classic images. You can have a person put on the flower and then have the father or mother of the groom to pretend to be putting on the flower. This may be a good time to take photos of the groomsmen together. It is also important to take a photo of the groom and his best man together. Look for parents of the bride and groom and introduce yourself. At this time I say to the parents, "the bride and groom would like your presence for formal photos after the ceremony".

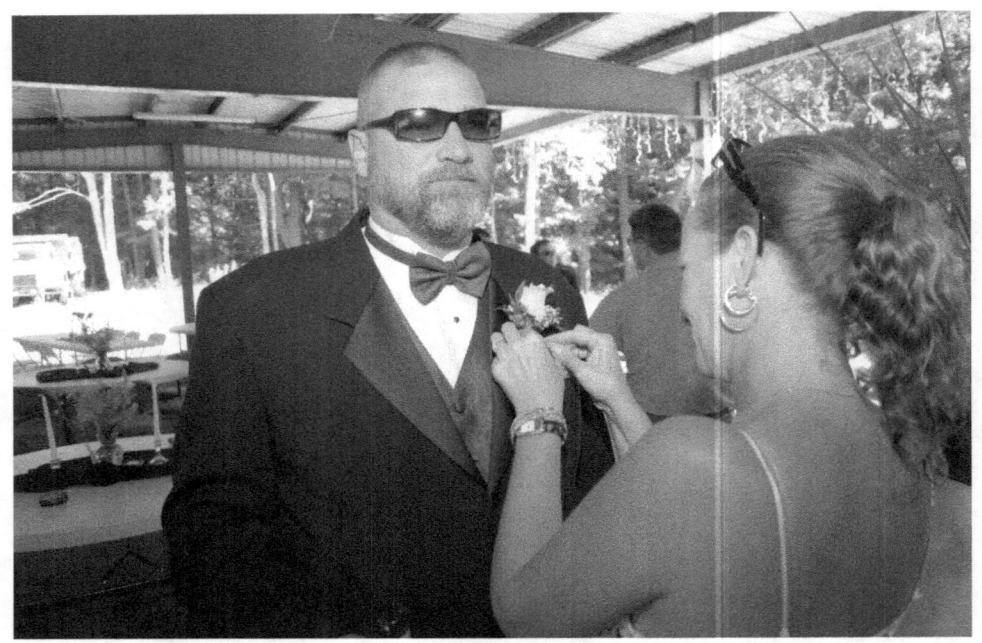

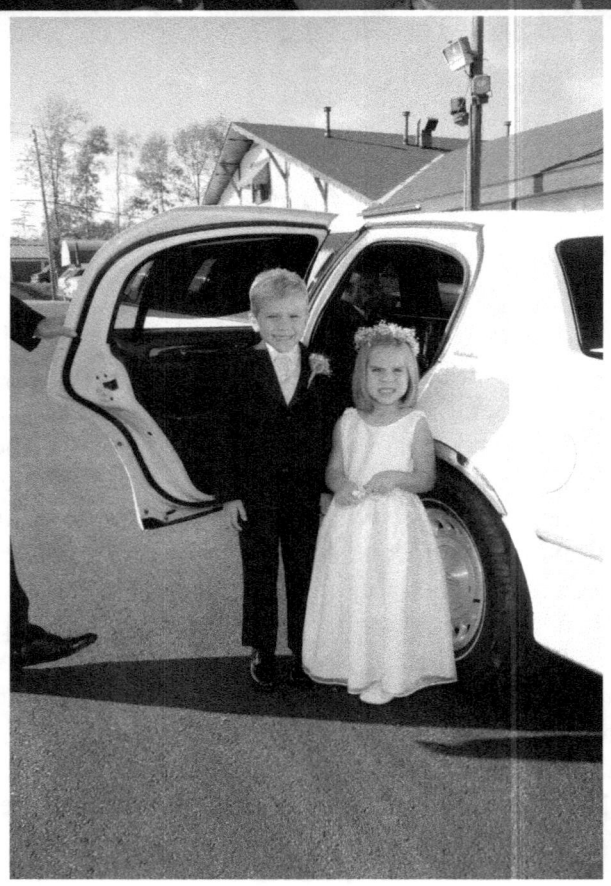

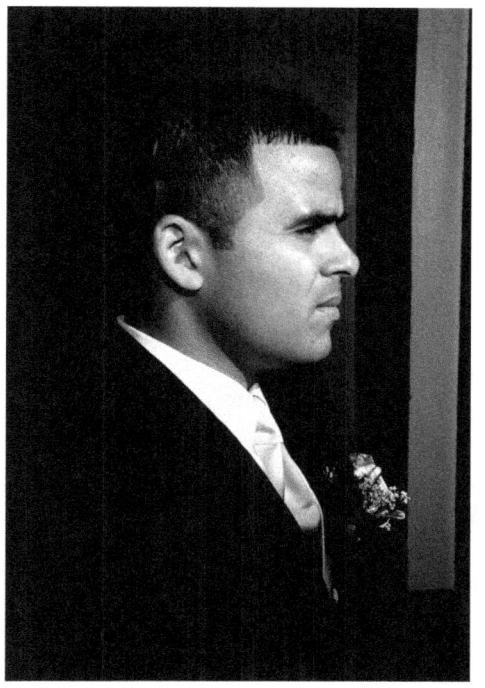

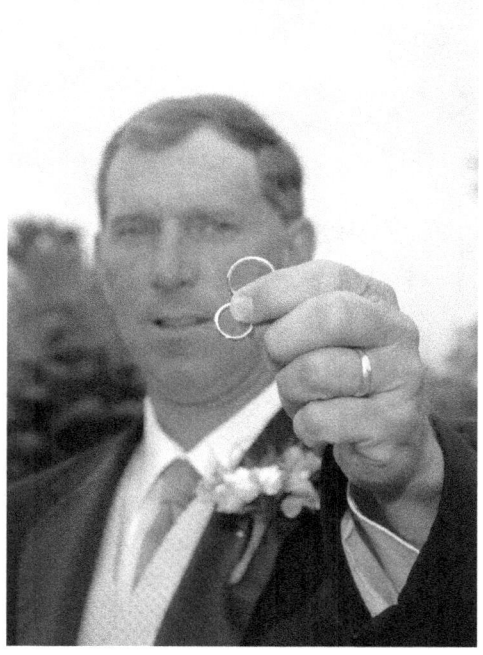

No flash, strong light from side window.

Full zoom to lower f-stop. Focus rings

Bounce flash

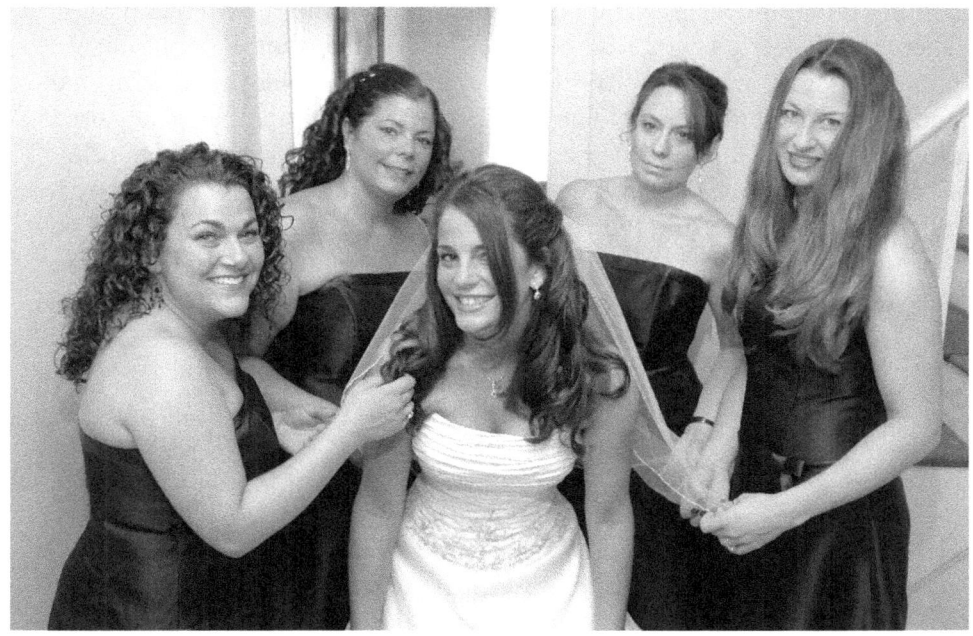

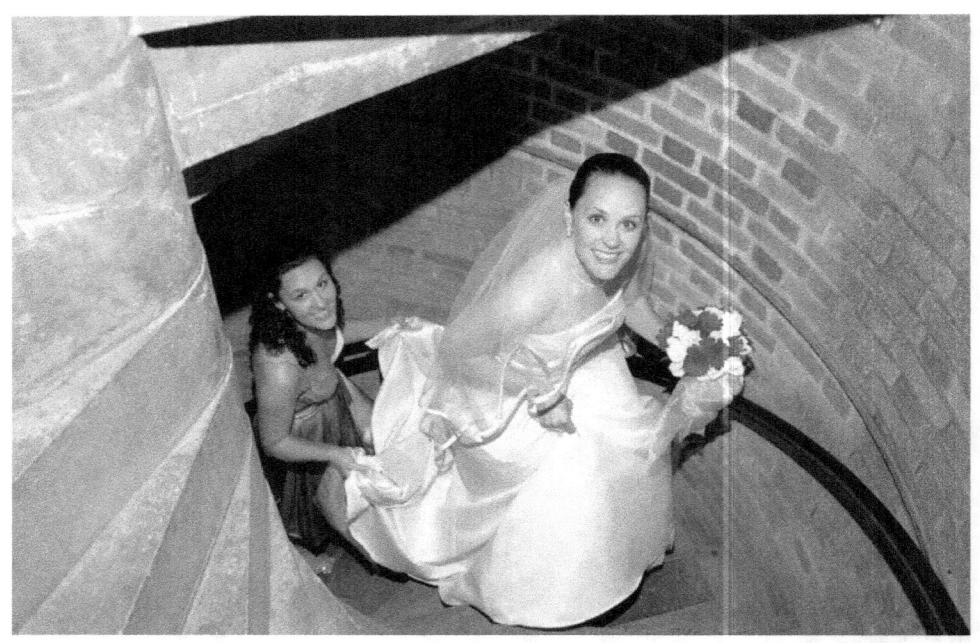

Ceremony

The ceremony usually starts with the escorting of mothers. Position yourself for isle shots. The groomsmen may be up at the altar or coming down the aisle. The brides party then comes down the aisle. Then the flower girl and ring bearer. Get down to their height when photographing, in addition try to get an image when they pass of all the guests using their camera. The next is the bride with father. Get some close up vertical and horizontal images. Pro tip stay to the brides side since she is usually shorter than the father or groom and is less likely to block an image. During the ceremony I try to stay as unobtrusive as possible. Take some basic close shots from different angles. In the beginning I usually walk to the back of the church to take a full wedding party photo. I then go back to the front and kneel down about two rows back. Take photos of important people taking part in the wedding also look for emotional shots among the guests. Photograph the exchanging of the rings. When the bride and groom kiss I usually stand to take this image, this is the most important image of the ceremony but if you miss it you can ask the bride and groom after the ceremony for a do over of the kiss. Carefully walk backwards down the aisle while photographing the bride and groom. Follow up with the rest of the wedding party and parents.

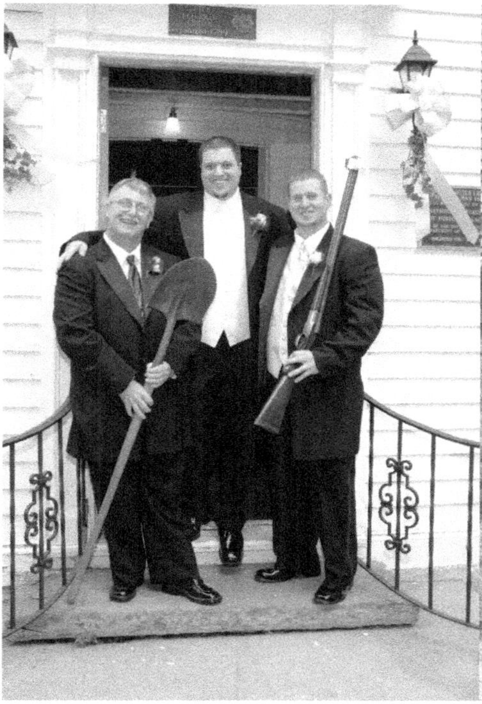

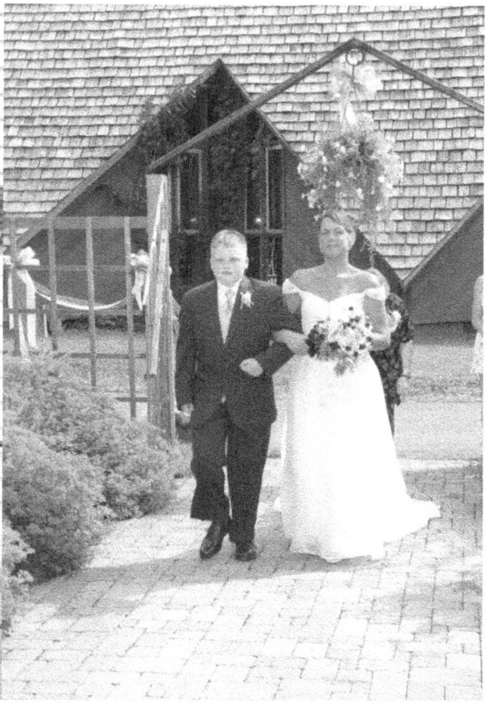

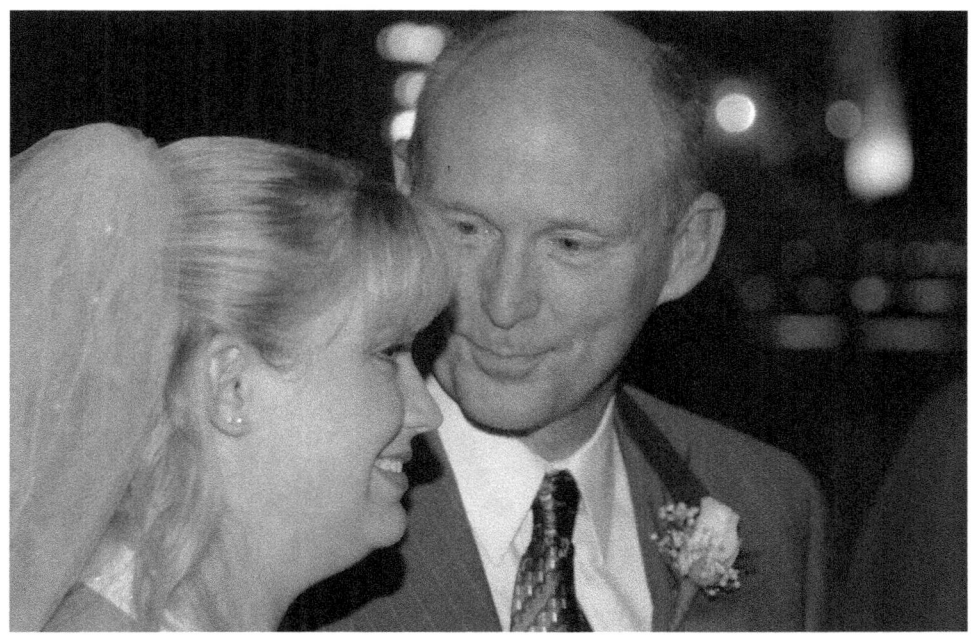

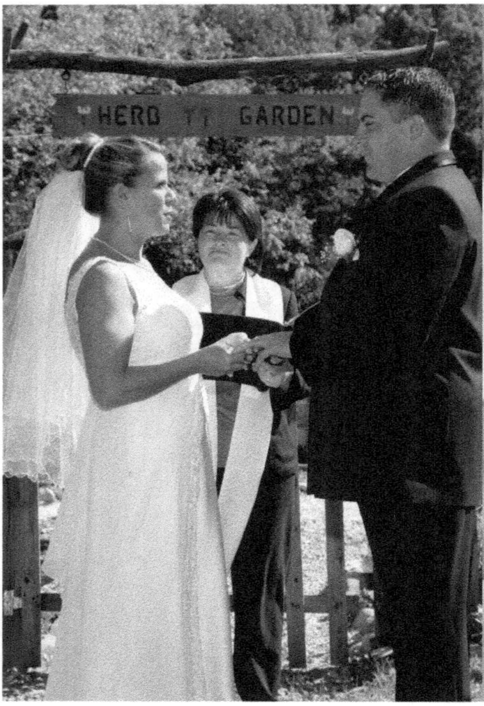

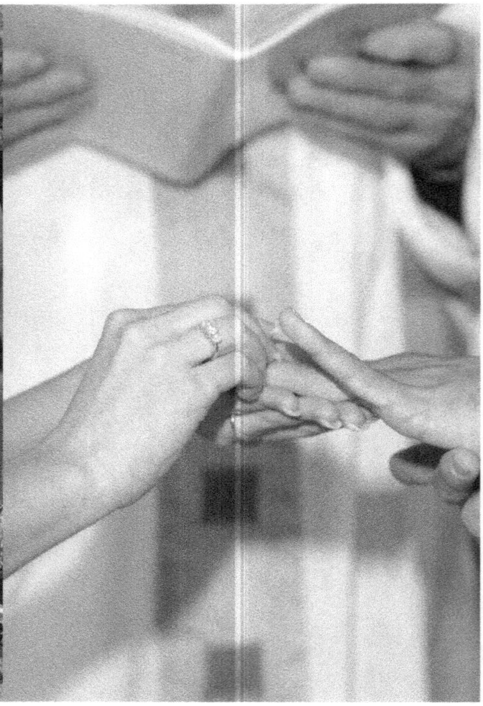

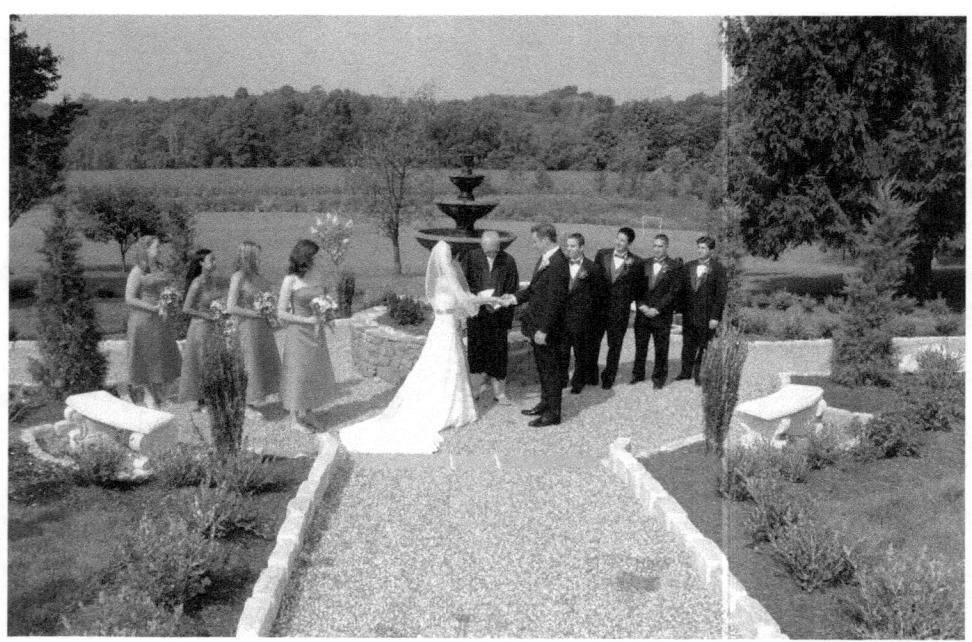

Notice the mid-range photo to an extreme close up and out to wide angle image.

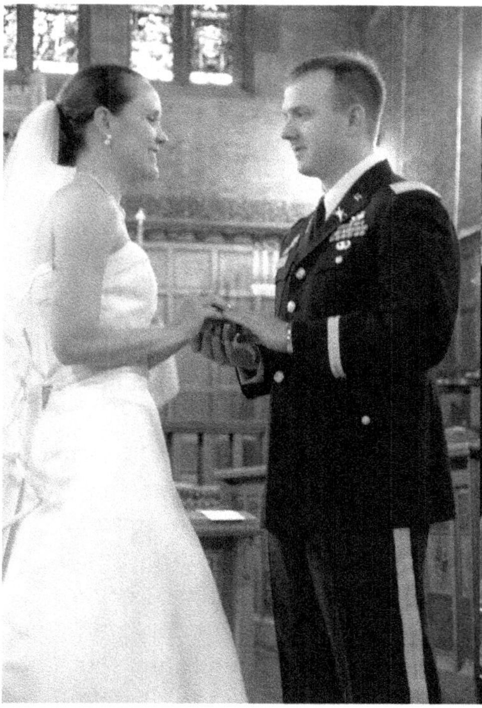

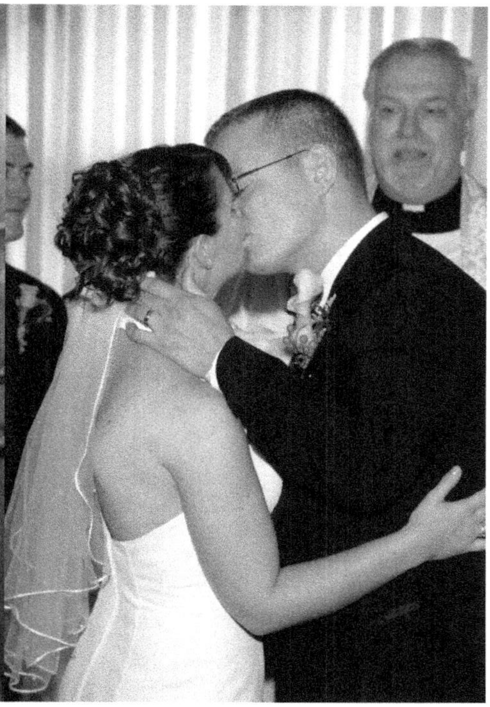

As long as the officiate doesn't mind go in for some discrete close-ups. Lower photo is a Butterfly release.

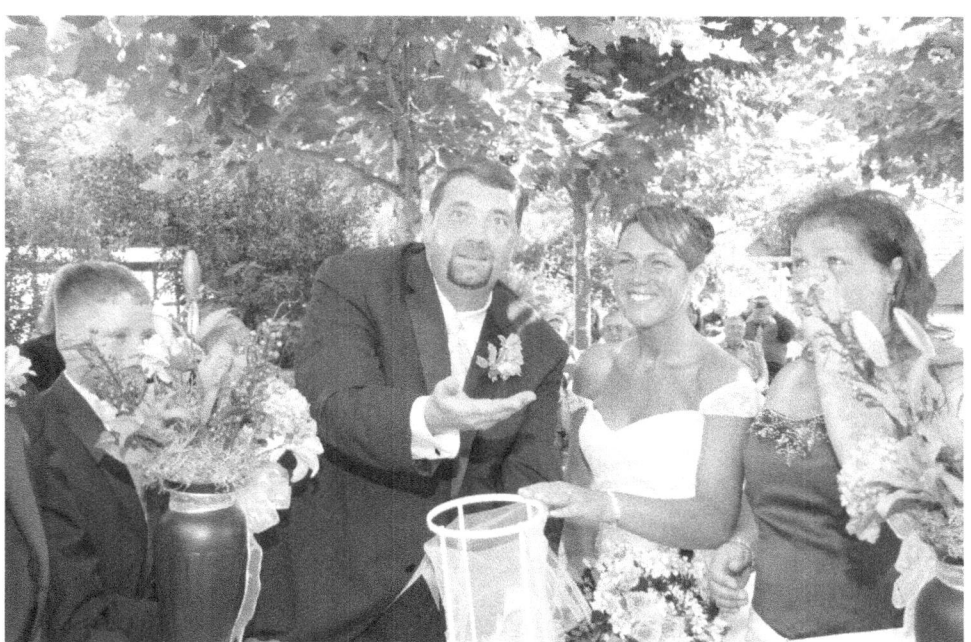

Formals

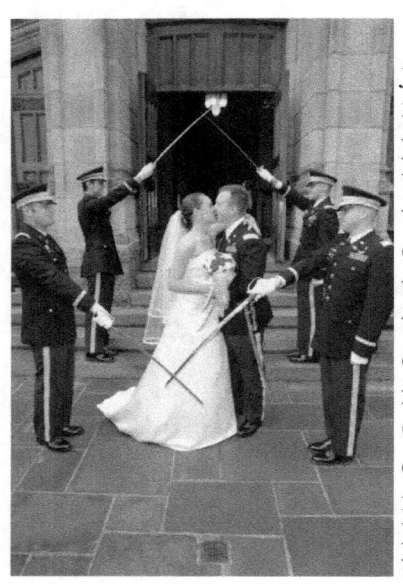

Many couples today want photo-journalistic style images. I still feel it is important to have some type of formal poses so that the significant people at the wedding are part of the images. Refer to the Shot Sheet that was created to be efficient. If important people are missing try to have a family member of the couple track them down. Do not allow the Bride or Groom to go in search of them, they will not make it back. Photos of the Bride and Groom can be taken while waiting for the other important guests. I like to keep all formals to a time period of twenty minutes. Remember that after the ceremony the bride and groom are entitled to a cocktail hour and then to the ceremony. Most of the wedding party would rather be at the cocktail hour and assuring them that these photos taken will be efficient will help with the overall cooperation.

I set up the bride and groom into a standard "thank you" card image. Making sure that the Grooms jacket is buttoned the way he wants and his flower looks good. You can tell which side the groom stands on because you can see his boutonniere. Bring the bride in and set down the dress. I usually ask the maid of honor to assist with the dress. Pay attention to detail. Ask the groom to relax his left arm. Once the basic pose is in place, don't move the bride and groom just simply add and remove family members.

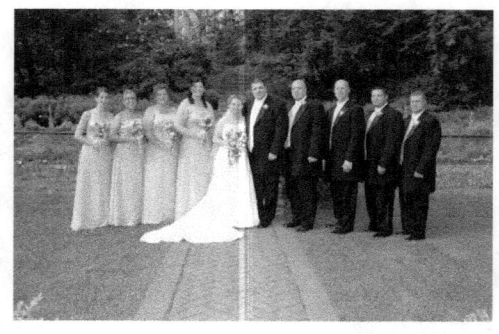

I usually start with the grandparents. This allows the older guests to go inside and relax at the cocktail hour. Lastly I add the entire wedding party for the full wedding party formal. What is important here is the even spacing. Make sure all of the men have the same buttons on their jackets. The Men's arms should be straight down and relaxed. Uniformity. Remind people about eyeglasses especially sunglasses. In addition make sure the women's flowers are all of the same height. After these photos, have the men step out and photograph the women with the bride. Have a solo image of the bride and her bridesmaid. Go to the grooms

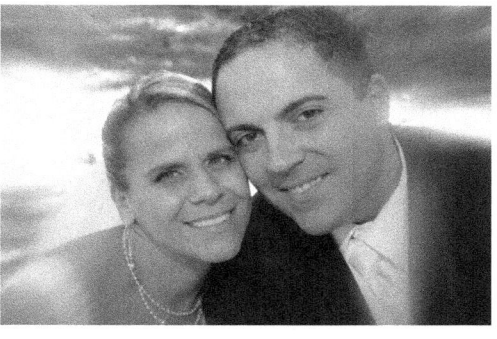

men and take an image of them with the groom. Take a groom and best-man photo. Excuse the wedding party except for the bride and groom.

Have some basic ideas for a couple's formals that look more cas-

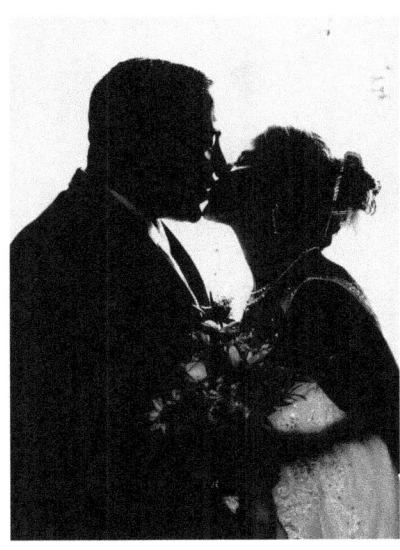

ual. Many of people that see my work, love my photojournalist style but many of these images are just what I consider casual formals. I set up the image but to not control fine point and allow some personality to show through. I step in if I belief the image may be unbecoming of the bride or groom. Try to create a flow to the order of poses, meaning if a bride is sitting take all of the sitting poses. In a couple of my poses I like to use a soft edge filter. The soft edge filter is done by purchasing another clear filter and placing a small amount of petroleum jelly in a circular motion on the very edge of the filter. Start with a wide circle and leaving the center of the filter clear. Have this filter ready before the wedding day and experiment at home with the size of the clear center. If there was an opportunity of a silhouette poses try to complete it now if not finish with the classic "ring shot".

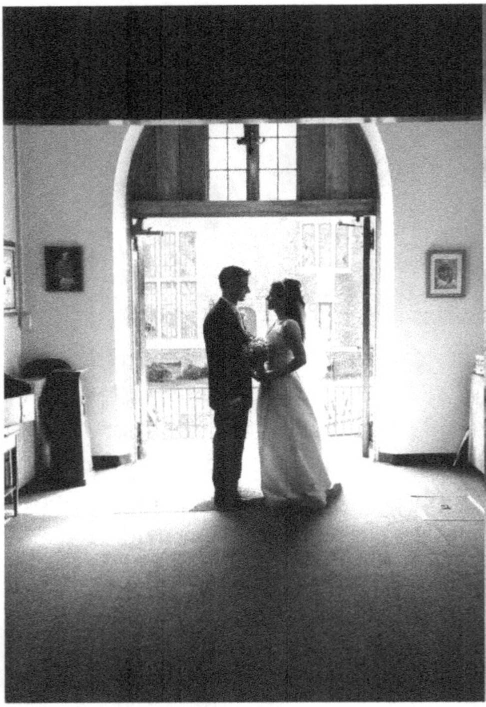

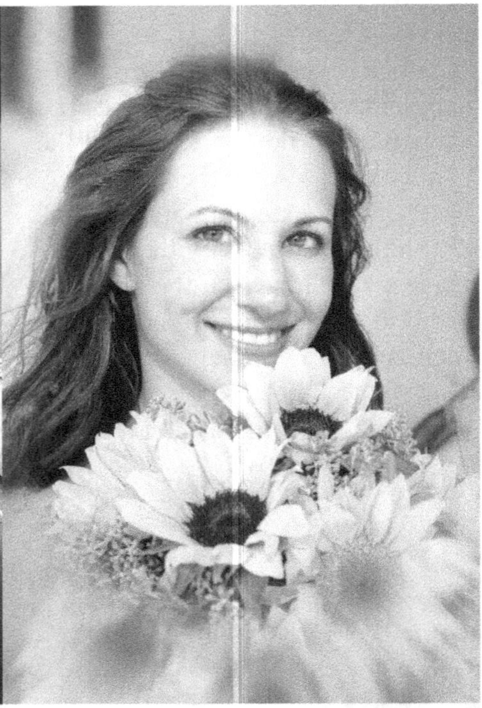

Camera is measuring strong outdoor light.   Soft edge filter

Extreme wide lens, don't use flash on main subject.

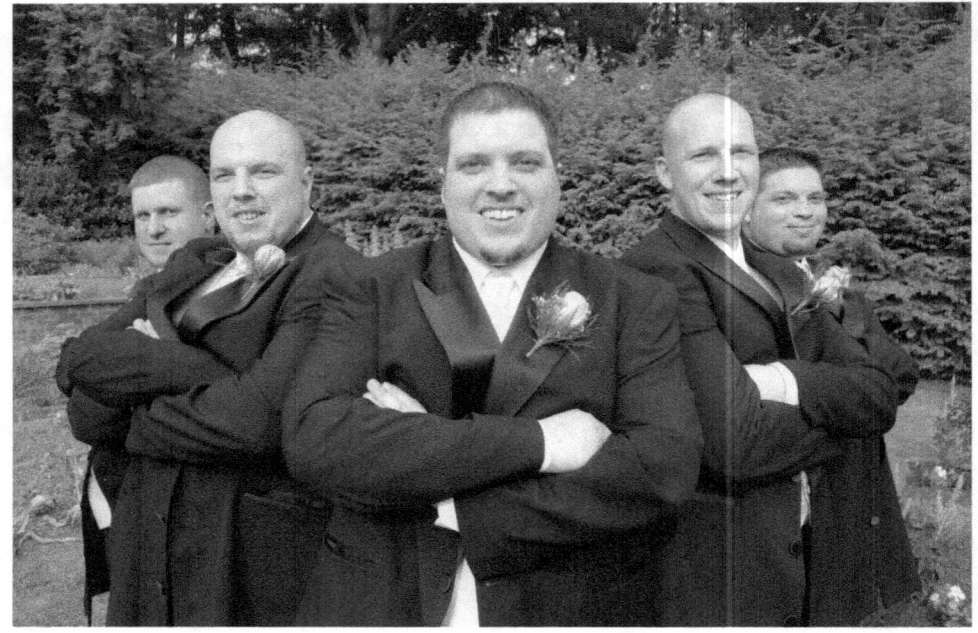

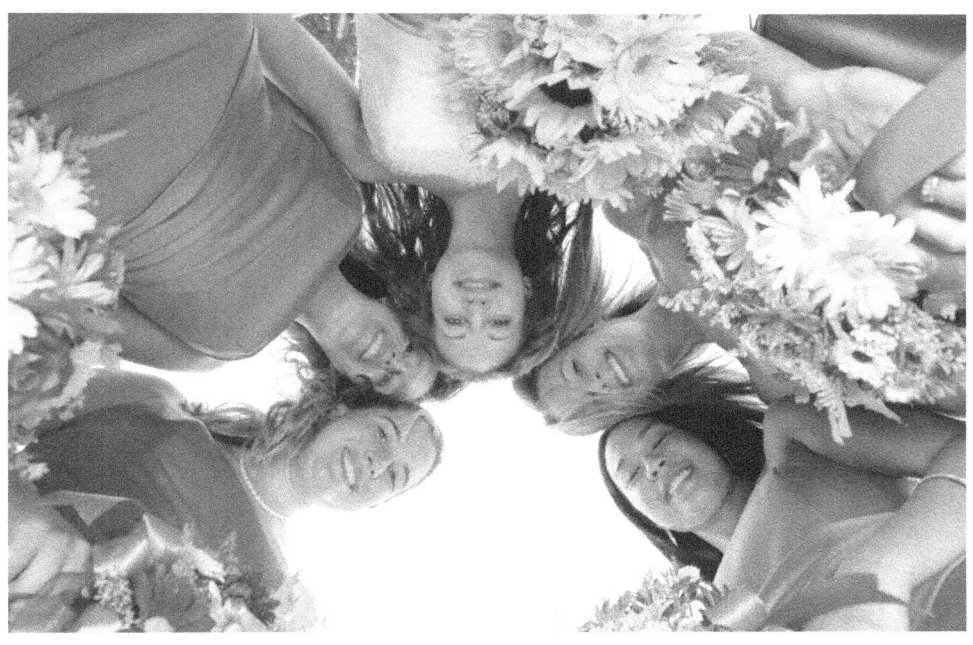

Laying on ground, shooting upward, need just a little flash.

Soft edge, cheek to cheek pose.

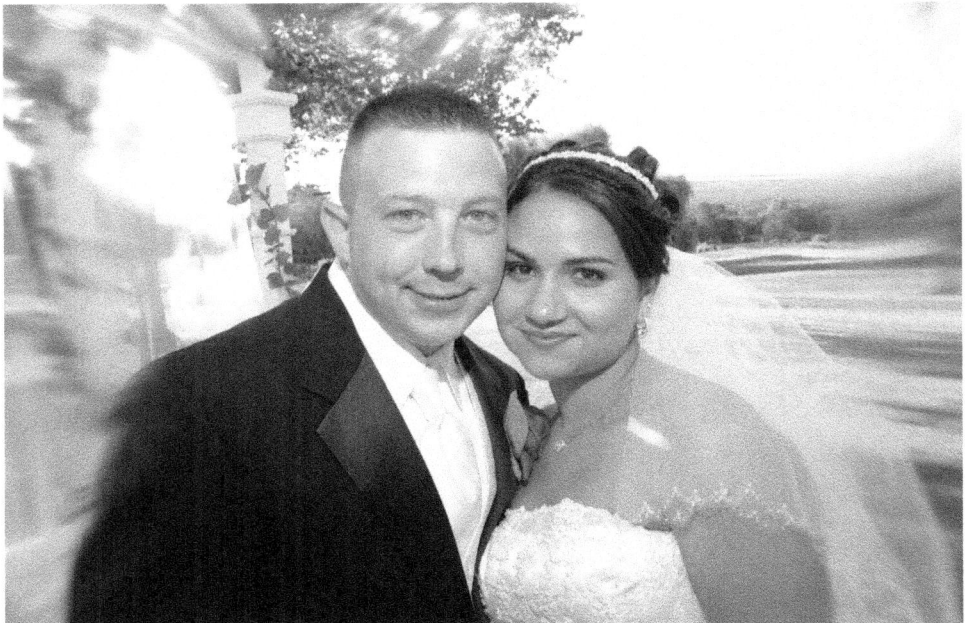

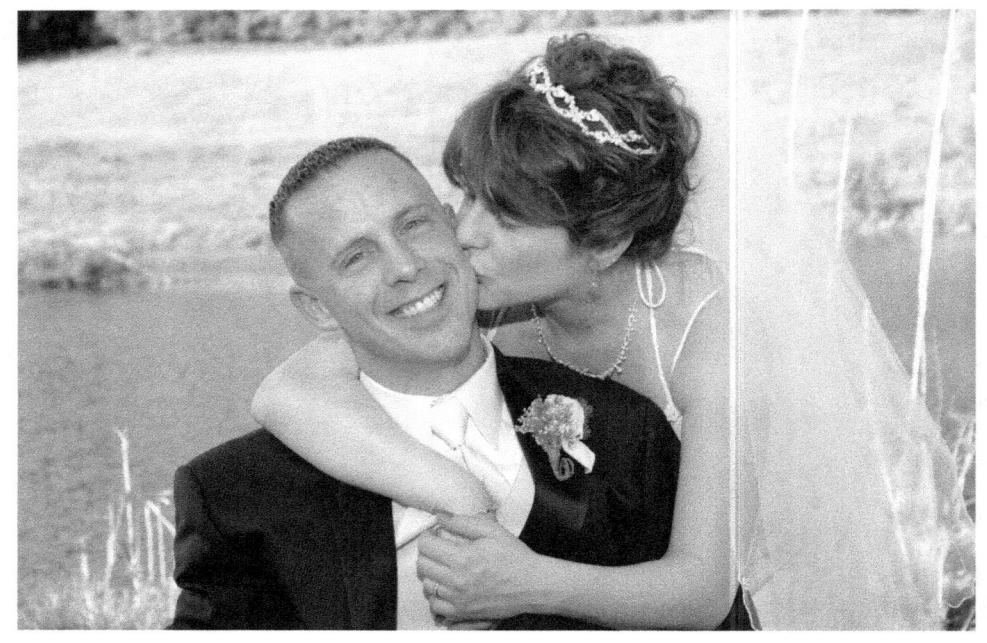

Groom seated

Groom seated, wide   Mid-range set up, harsh backlight, no flash

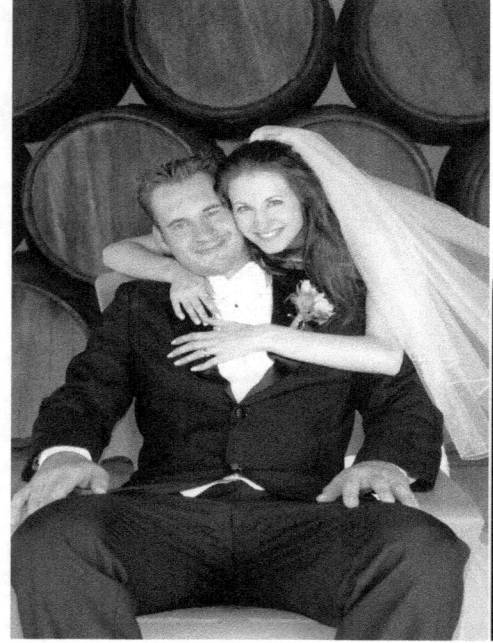

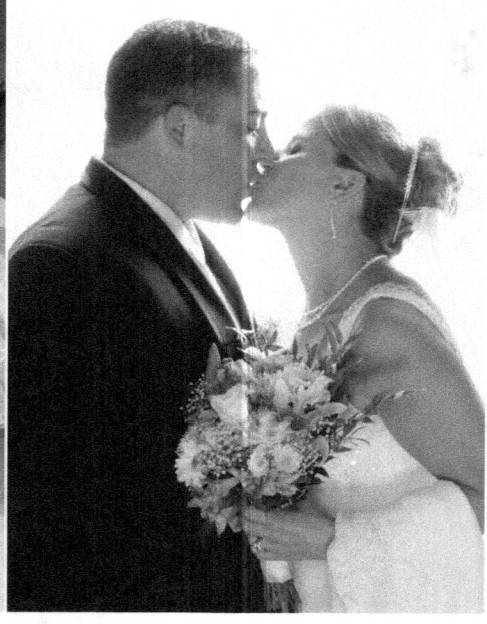

Cocktail Hour

During this hour you must get your equipment to the reception area. First take an image of the place cards for each guest before they come into the room. It would also be a good time to take an image of the entire dining room. Then go in for a close up of the table setting, Invitation and gift. This is a good time to meet with the DJ and ask him the order he is going in or any special request of the wedding party that you should be aware of.

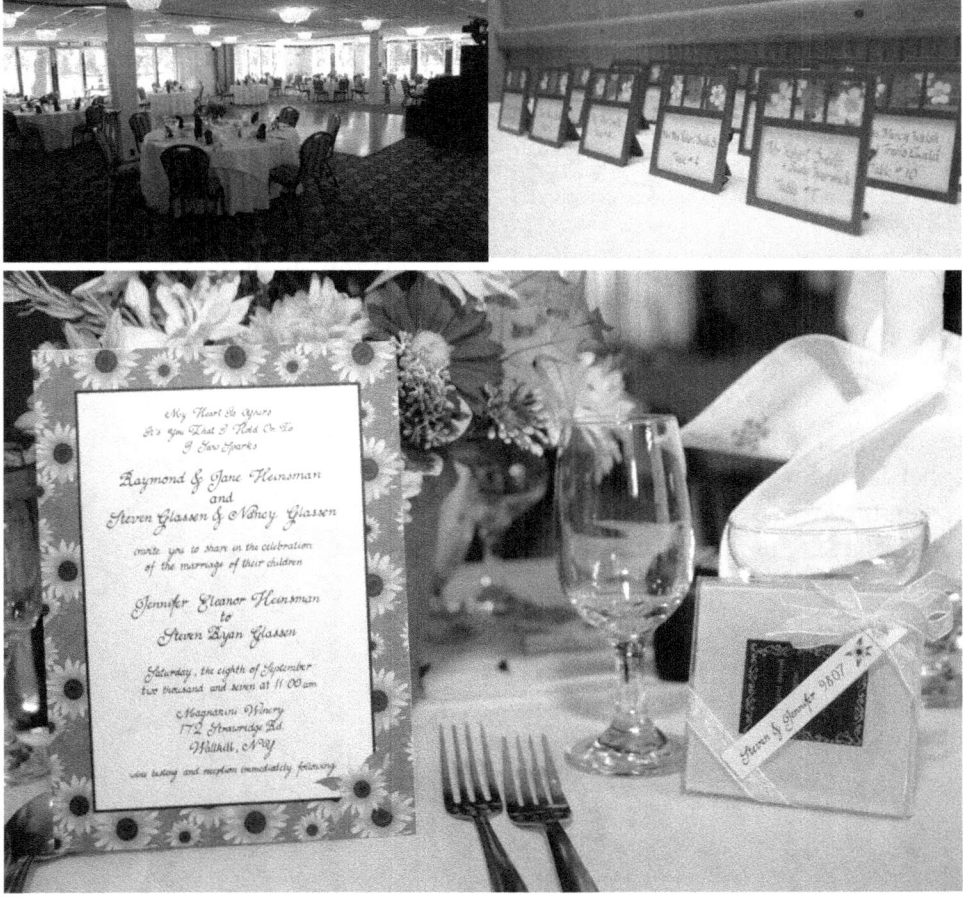

Reception

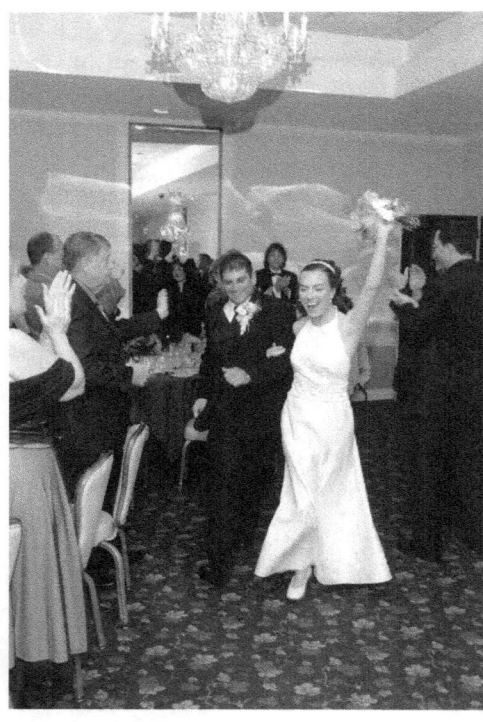

Prepare for the DJ to start the introductions of the wedding party. Immediately following is the first dance by the bride and groom to their wedding song. Take a Dance pose photo. Step back and take some wide angle photos. Sometimes the parent dances are next. Ask for a quick pose and step back allowing them to dance. There is usually many emotional photo images during this time. Giving them some space will allow better images. After these dances everyone will sit down and the best man will give his speech. Try to have the best man with his glass stand near the newlyweds. The catering hall will now start to bring in the first course. This is a good time to attempt the table shots. Be aware of elderly people and have them stay seated while the other half of the table stands behind them. The center piece my need to be removed. Table shots can be challenging but it is the best way to guarantee that everyone in attendance has been photographed. When the main course is served, this is usually the biggest break for the photographer in the evening. The catering hall usually has a table set up out of site. Put your camera gear in a safe area near you and take a break.

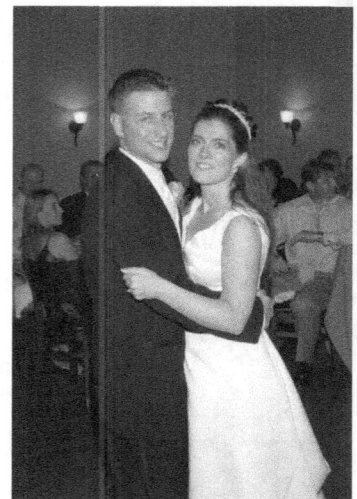

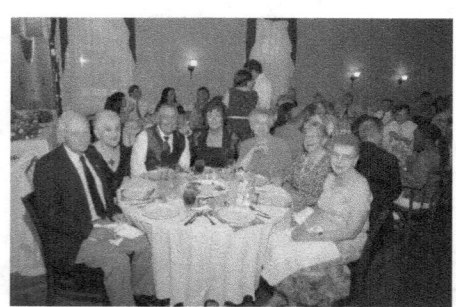

Pay attention to the DJ, usually they will run the event.

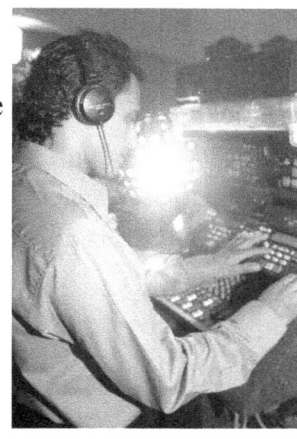

When most of the guest have completed the main course, the party starts. Pay attention to the music arrangement. Slow songs give the best opportunity for couples photos. If the DJ is having a good crowd on the floor he will be less likely to slow it down. Look for great moments and let them happen. Zoom in and out while taking photos. In addition try to get photos from higher angles. Some photographer use a step ladder for this purpose. I usually hold the camera high above my head to achieve this height. The dancing will be interrupted about an

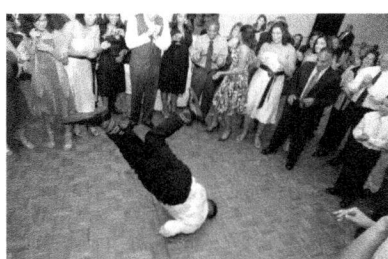

hour before closing to cut the cake. Some catering halls will set up the couple for this cake cutting photo. If not make sure that the bride or groom's face is not blocked. Get a photo of them holding the knife looking at you and a couple of photos of them looking down at the cake. Let them cut the cake and serve each other. Next is the garter ceremony. The bride will sit down while the groom removes the garter from the brides leg. All the single women will gather on the floor and the bride will toss her mini bouquet. The groom will have all of the single men on the floor catch the garter. The woman with the bouquet will take a seat and the man with the garter will put the garter on the woman leg.

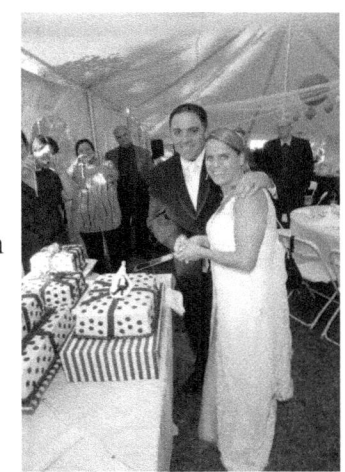

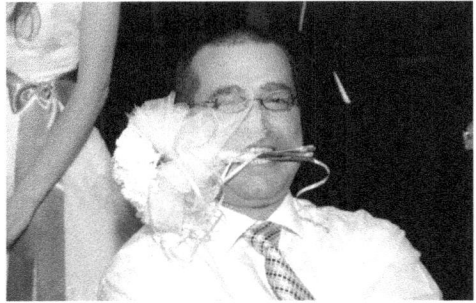

It is a good idea to have the people that caught the items take a photo with the bride and groom. The cake will now be delivered and it is back to dancing. Some of the guests will start to leave. The Bride and groom will usually be saying there good byes.

buys. The wedding photographer usually also leaves at this time. Before packing up, say good bye to the bride and groom. Mention when the photos will be complete. Sometimes the bride needed a photo with a person and forgot until this moment. If you stay until the end there will usually be a last dance song. Make sure to say good bye to the DJ and Maître Dee. Usually there is an exchange of business cards at this time.

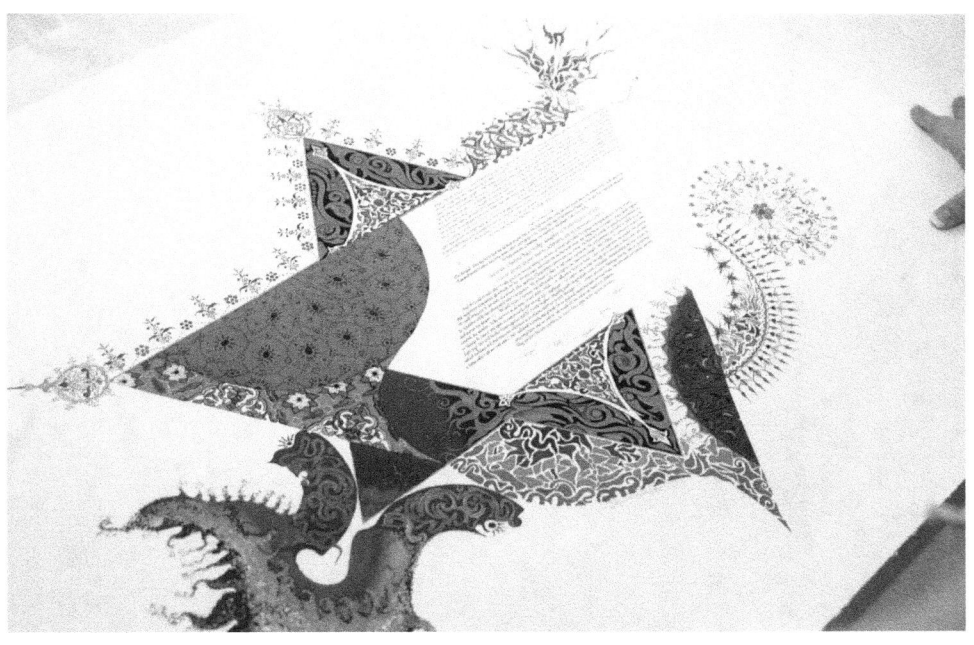

Ketubah, Jewish wedding contract

Always take cake photo early on   SILOHOUTTE

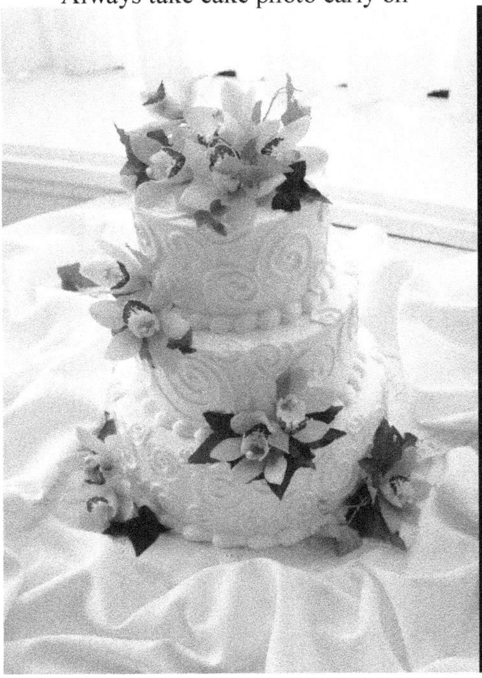

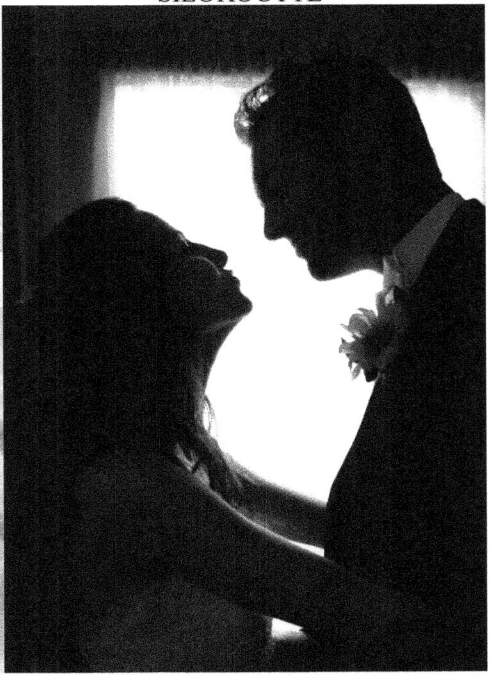

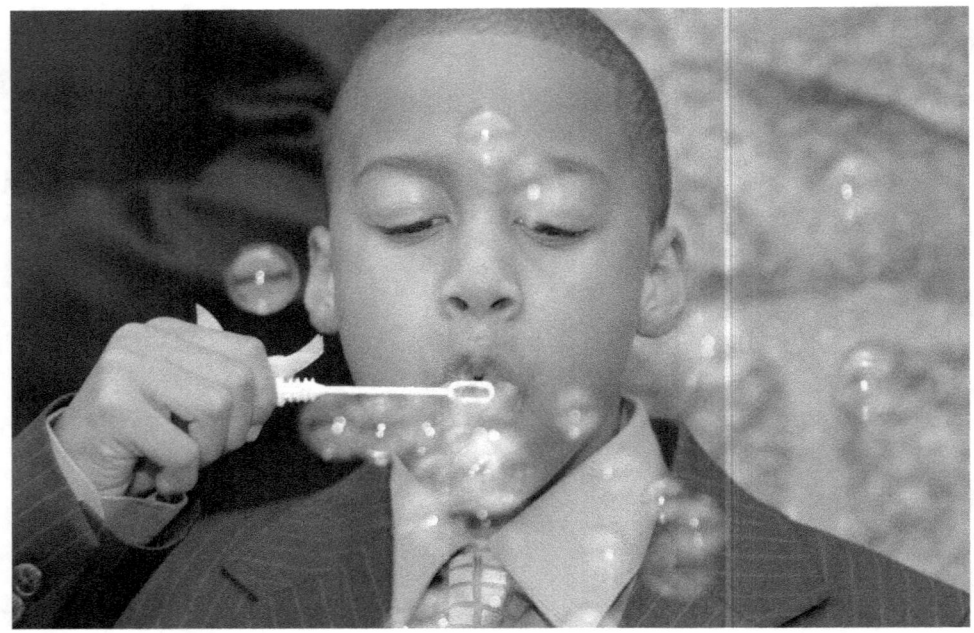

Extend zoom all the way out and focus on subject, it lowers f-stop.

Outdoor seated photo but taken in the shade of a tree.

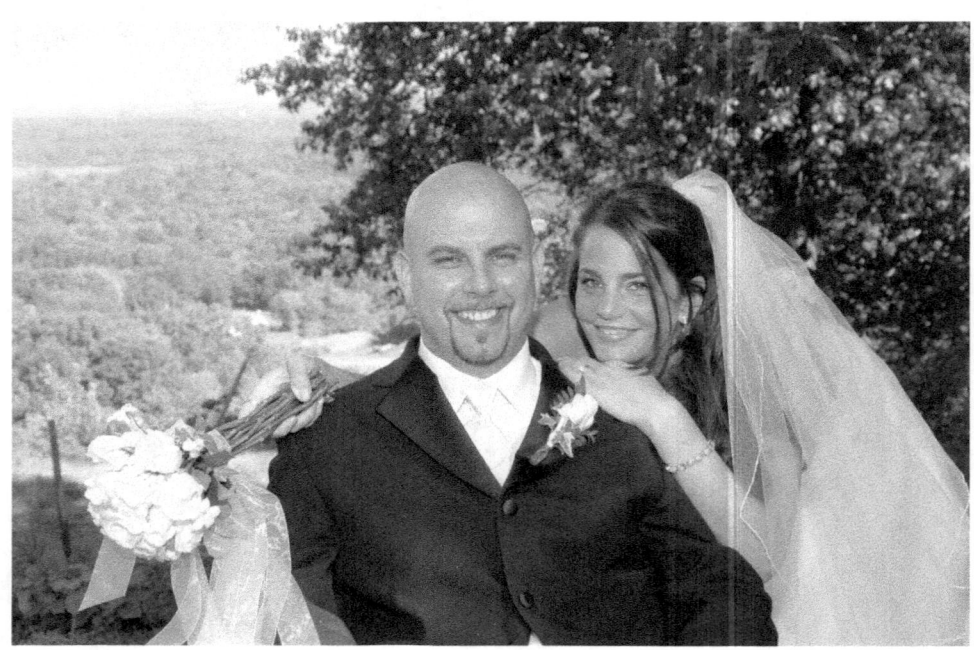

Groom stands behind and grabs waist of bride on other side. Notice that these photos are taken in the shade of a tree.

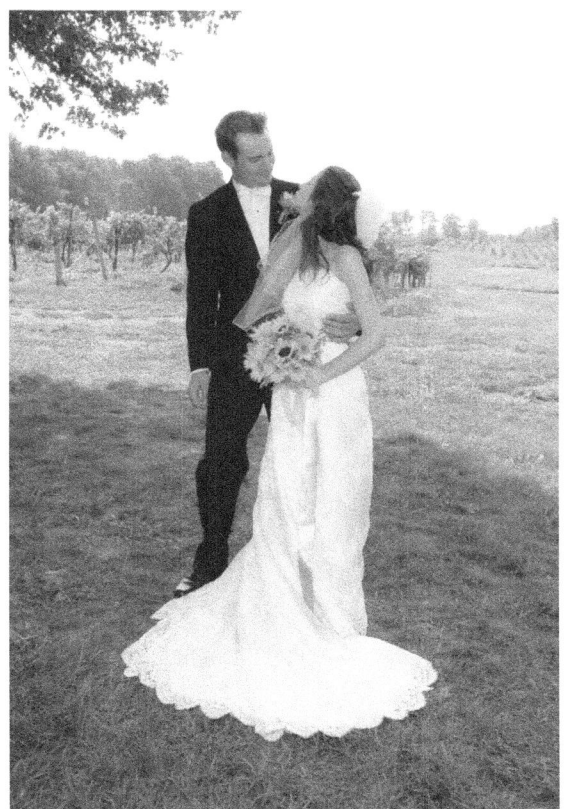

Reflection of mirror.

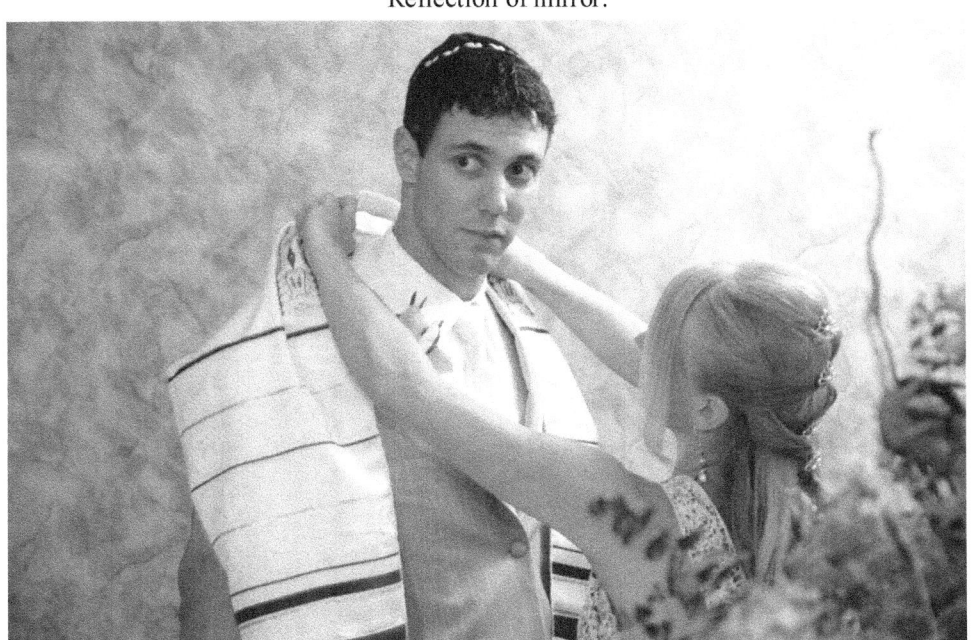

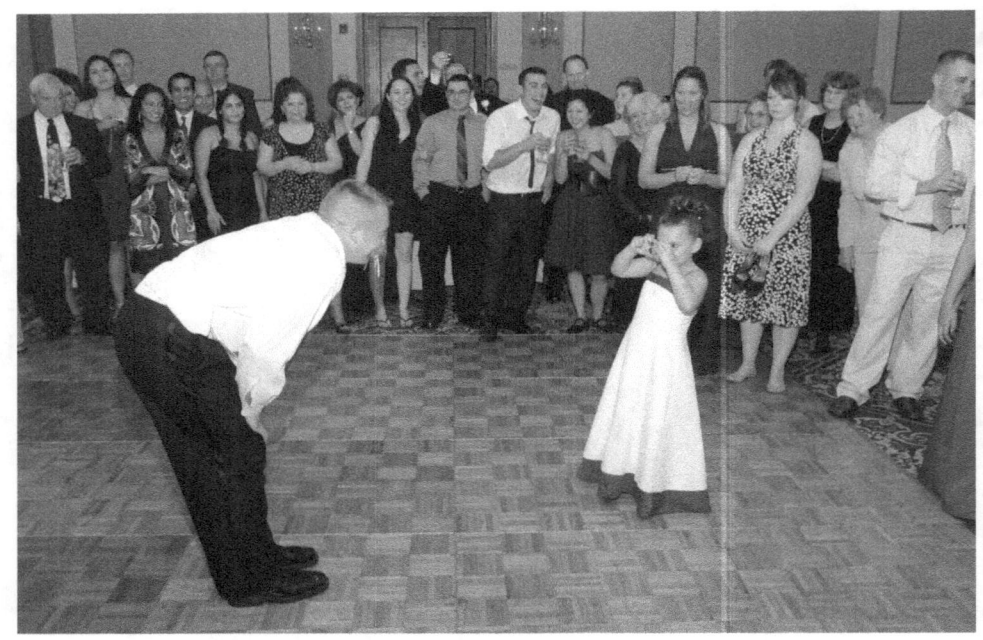

Child holding a camera.

A lot of work went in to these chairs, so I am sure that the couple would like a photo .

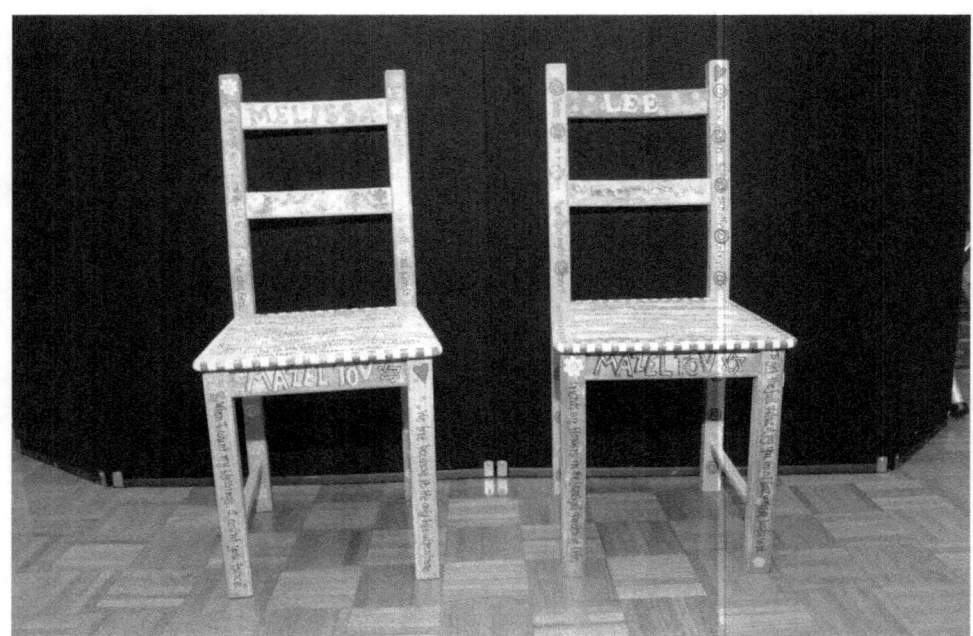

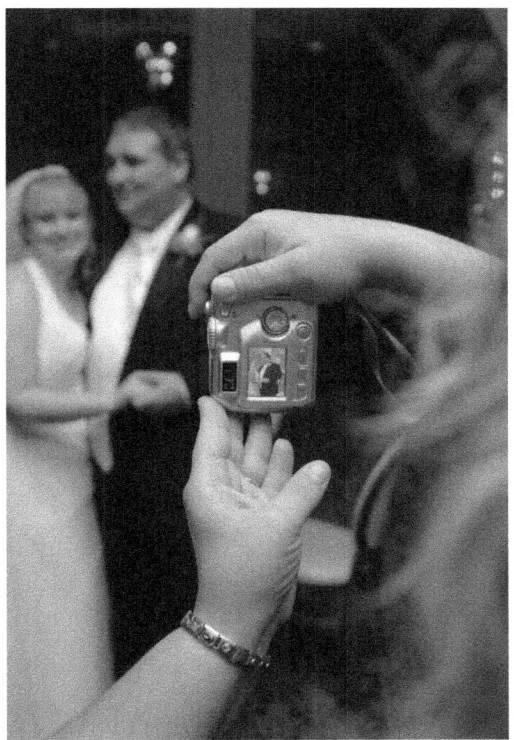

Have someone take a photo of the bride and groom while you focus on the image of the point and shoot camera. It makes a great framing photo. Try to keep the bride and groom in the background.

Lower Photo, this is my signature poses. I take multiple photos close-ups and wide, them looking at me and each other.

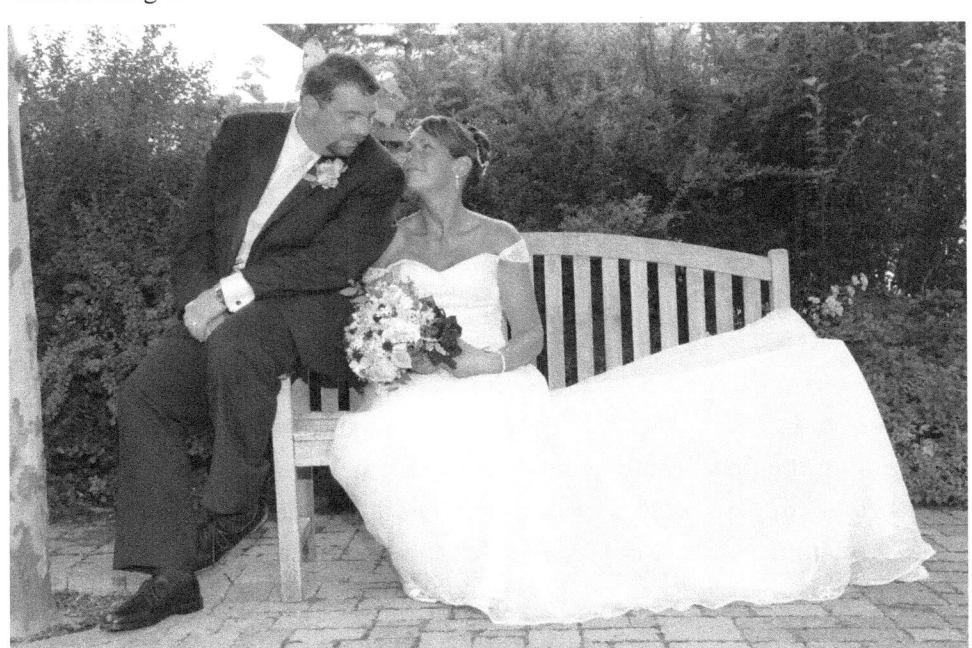

AFTER THE WEDDING

Take the camera home and immediately take the photo memory card and make a copy onto a separate media. This is vital. The photos should always be in at least two separate places. What I mean by a separate media is that the photos are uploaded to the computer's hard drive and are also on the memory card. Before erasing the memory card the photos must be copied to another media like a data DVD. I usually also upload them to an online photo processing website. Try to keep your own personal copy of each wedding on a data DVD for possible future needs.

Photo Editing

Keep the original upload to the hard drive untouched. Create another copy and put it into another folder to be edited, this way you can also go back to the original if there is a mistake. The best way to correct an images exposure is by editing the "curves" in the photo editing software. Secondary by bumping up the images in brightness and contrast. Hopefully most of the images are composed well but if not there could be a need for some cropping. When cropping try to fill the frame. Most importantly to remember is that these photos will most likely be printed in a 4" by 6" print. The cropped image must be in this rectangle shape or the processing center will over crop the image.

Final Products

I always like to copy the entire wedding to a DVD data disk for the bride and groom. I usually use Lightscribe that burns an image directly on to the disc. Many couples enjoy memory books, these are images printed directly in to a book form. There are also many options for thank you cards. Check out www.WeddingPhotographerBook.com for more ideas.

Conclusion

Get out there and use your camera. When I started with the idea of starting my own wedding photography business many people would say that if it was that easy everyone would be doing it. After year of photographing weddings, I am surprised that everyone is not doing it. I feel that the issue is that people are intimidated by the idea of it. When you sit back and look at the big picture, it is not intimidating. Most of the day, the photographer is working as a journalist, photographing the flow of events. The photographers primary responsibility is setting up the formals that many couples today are asking less of. I have a well prepared shot list of poses that helps elevates that issue. Imagine having a career as wedding photographer were work is party. Have fun!

Thank you for reading my book and please check out my website,

www.WeddingPhotographerBook.com

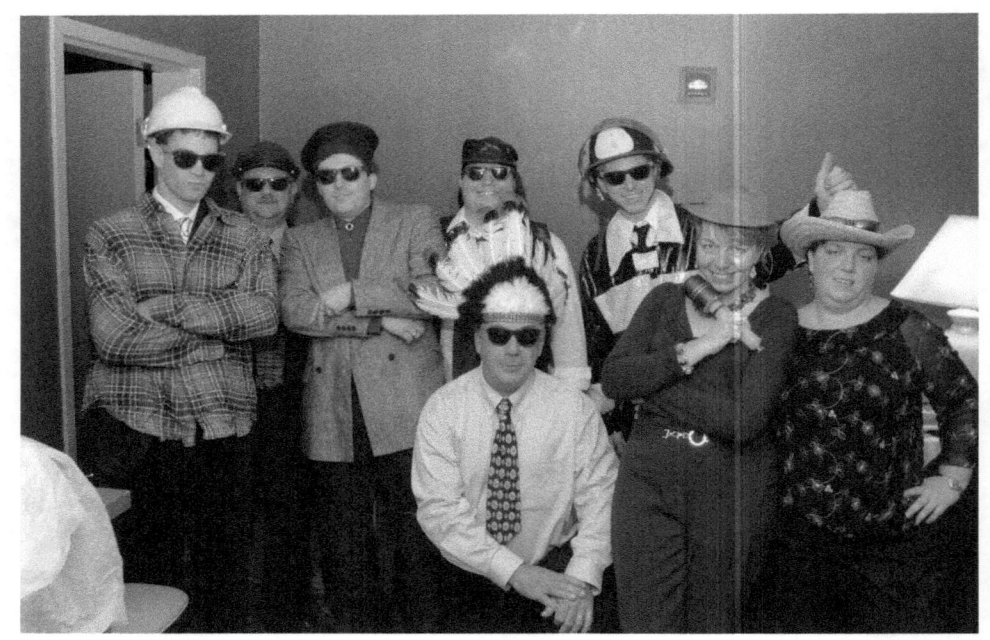

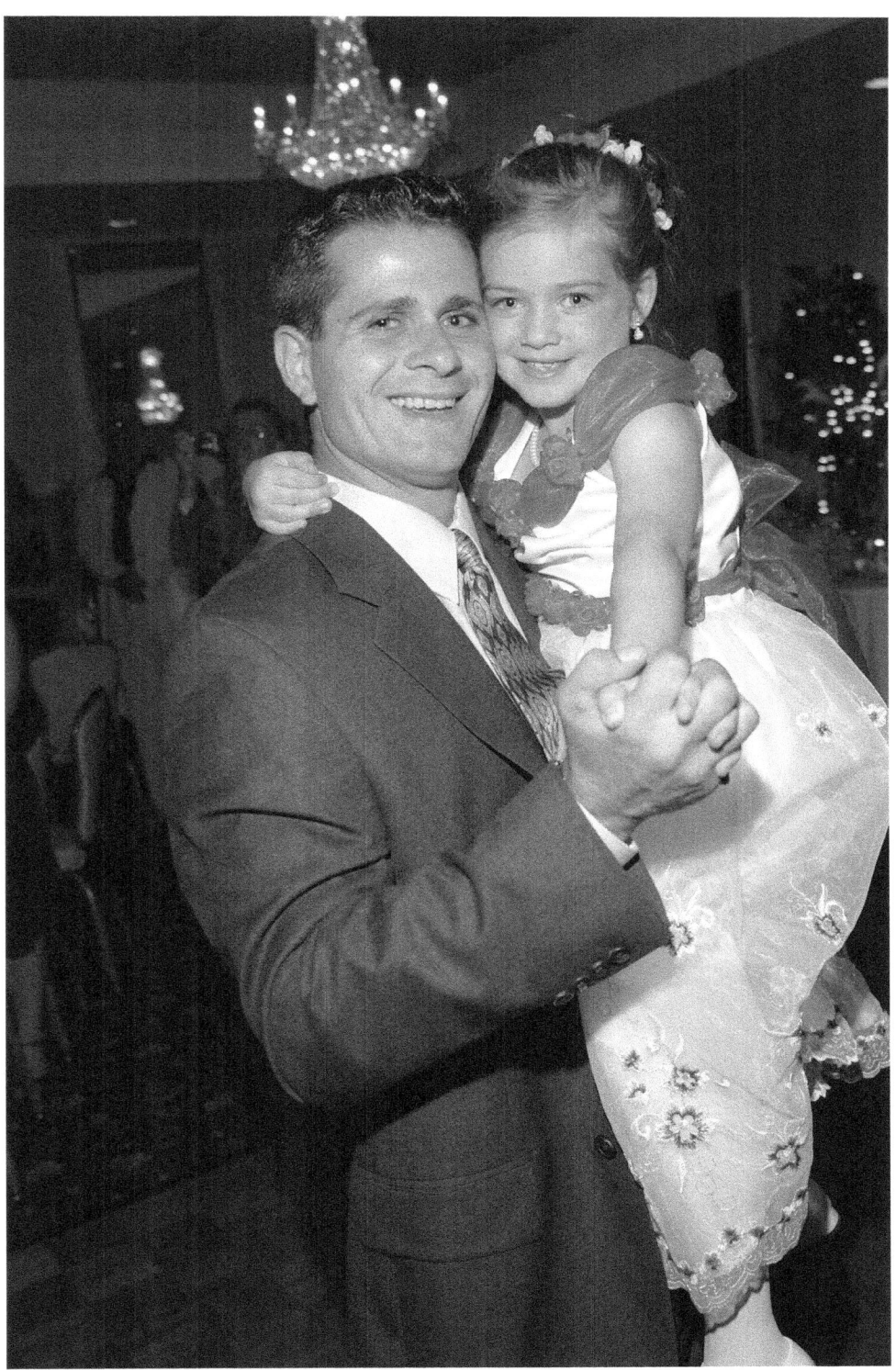

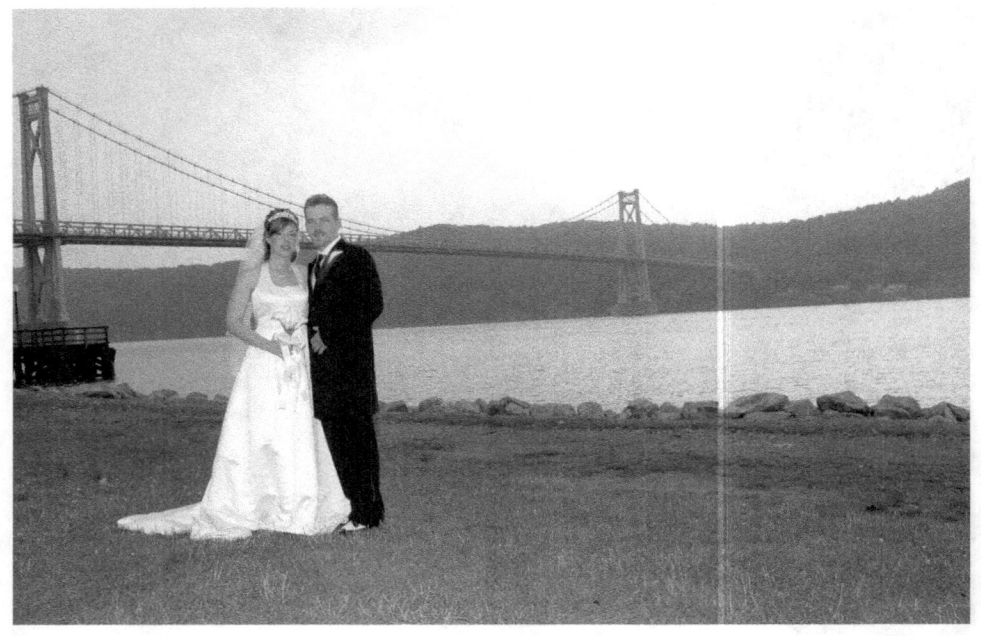

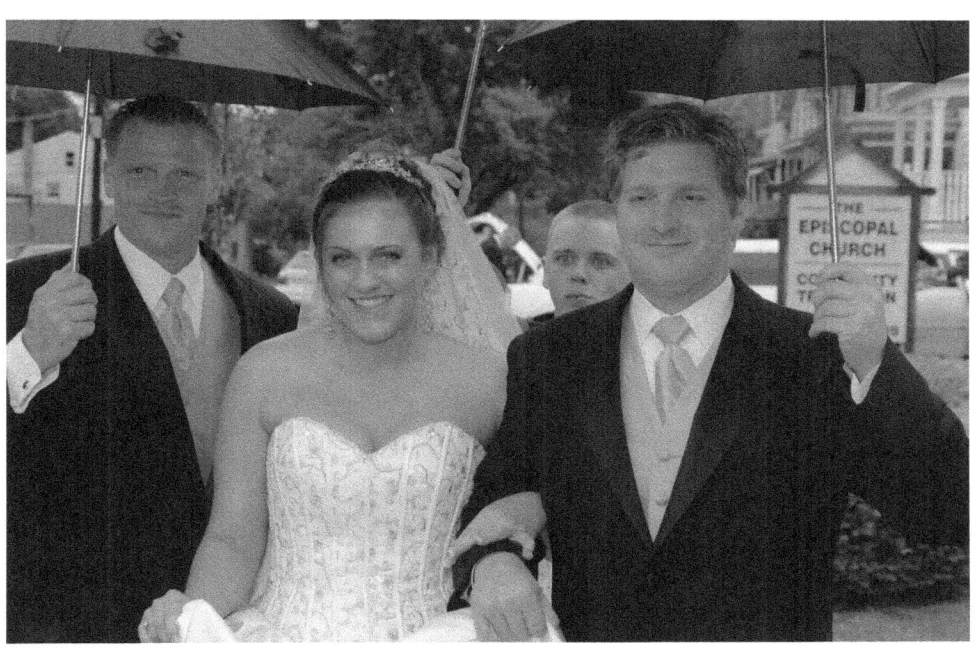

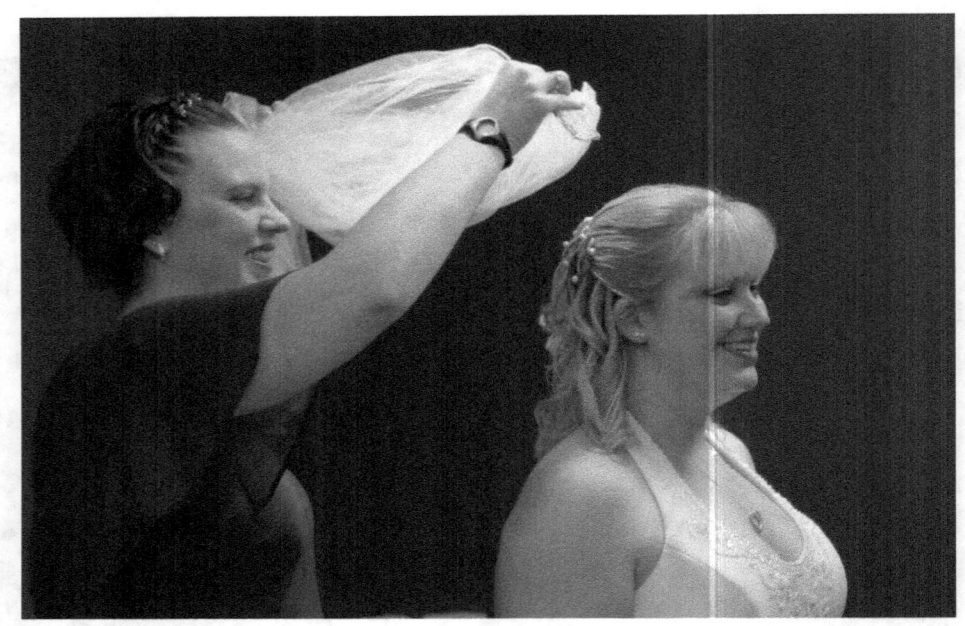

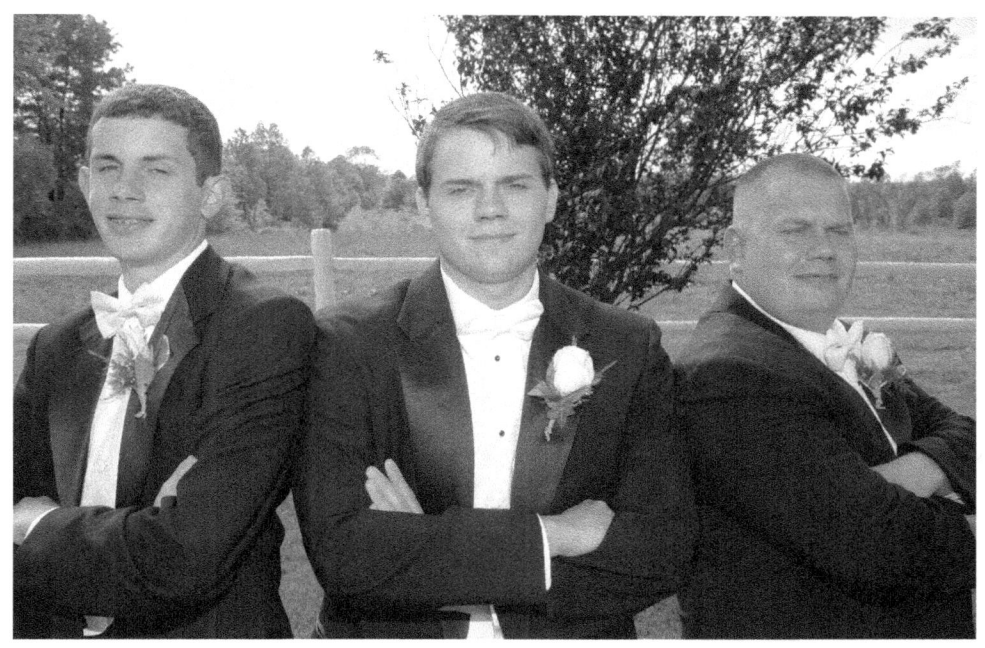

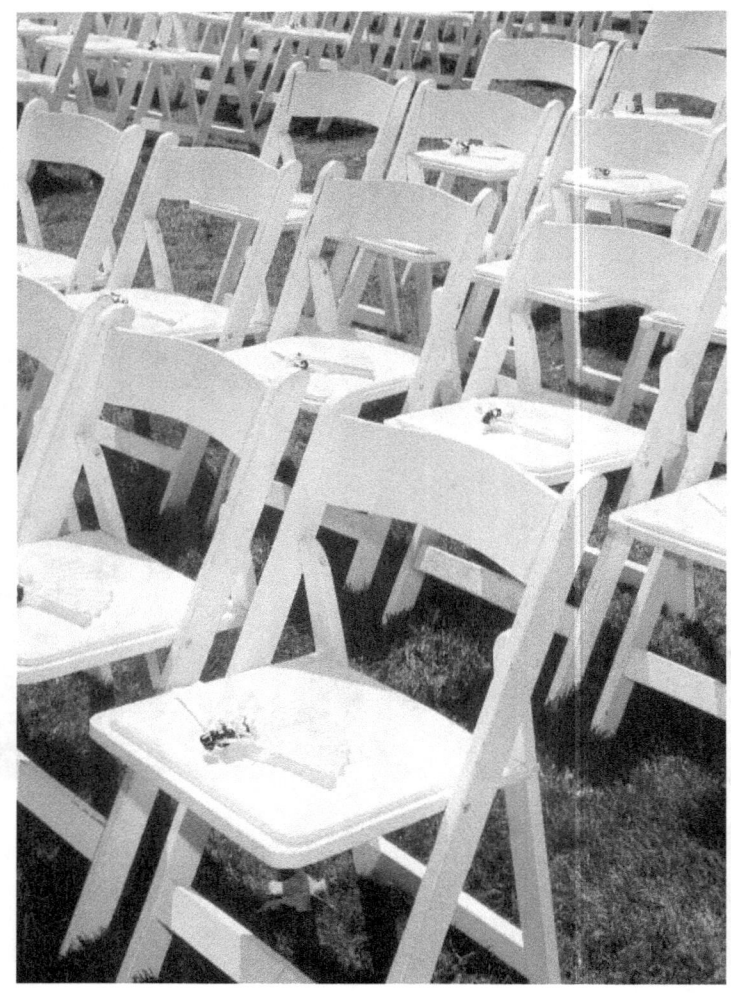

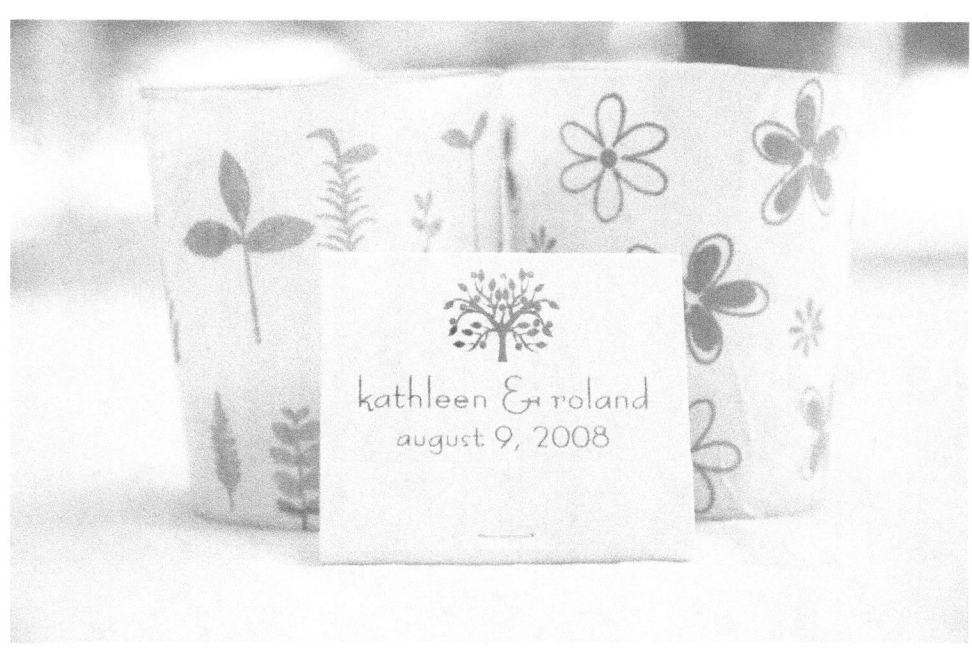

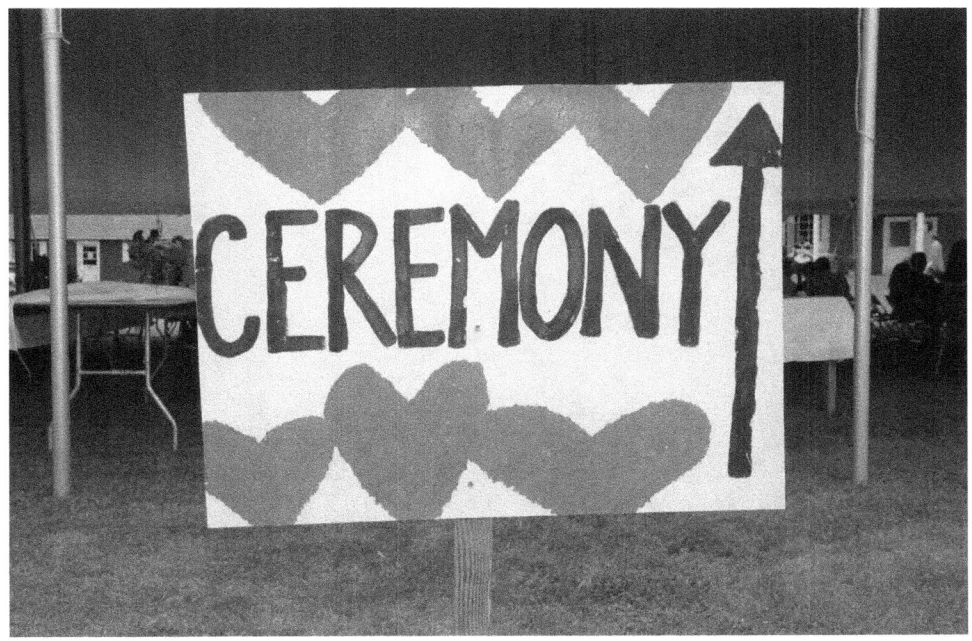

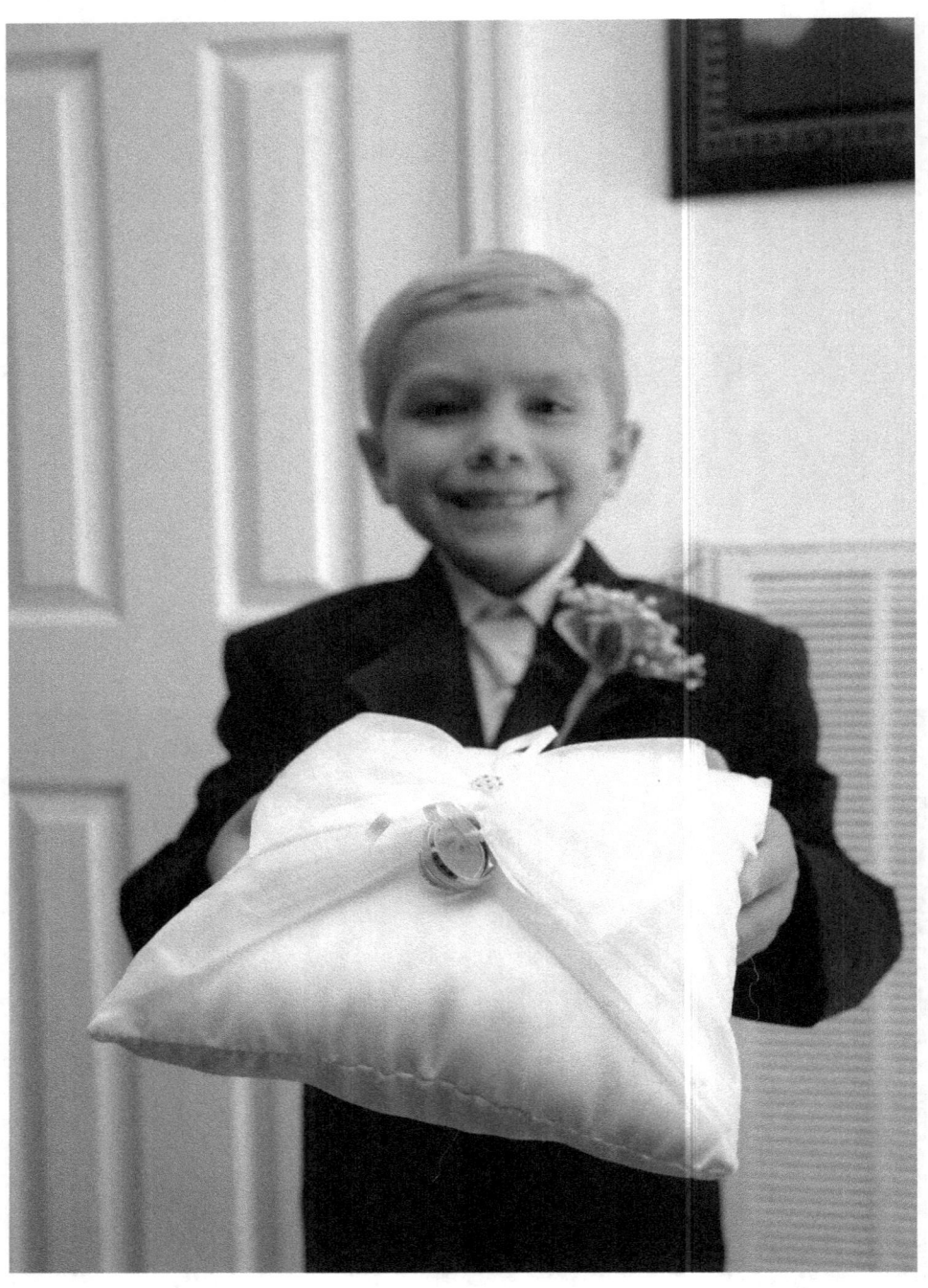